June Meyer's Authentic Hungarian Heirloom Recipes

By June V. Meyer & Aaron D. Meyer

Second Edition

Second Printing November 1999

Published by Meyer & Associates
978 Maple Ct. Deerfield, Illinois 60015
(847) 945-5358
E-mail: june4@interaccess.com
Web Site: http://homepage.interaccess.com/~june4/

ISBN: 0-9665062-0-0

LCCN: 98-162177

Dedication

This book of Heirloom Hungarian Recipes is dedicated to preserving the memories and recipes of my mother Theresa Rose Sehne Wischler, and my father, Frank John Wischler.

It could not have been done without the immense encouragement, computer knowledge and help of my son, Aaron David Meyer.

"What was once lost, is now found."

Foreword by June Meyer

The writing out of these recipes and stories were accomplished over a two and a half year period, from March 1995 to December 1997. It entailed countless hours of work sitting at computers.

These recipes were originally posted on the Internet in my Home page entitled "June Meyer's Authentic Hungarian Recipes" It grew from twenty recipes to over ninety six.

This collection of old family recipes reached more than 150,000 people around the world as of November, 1999 through the Internet. I have received over a thousand e-mail letters from Hungarians, descendants of Hungarians, descendants of Austrian-Hungarians, descendants of German settlers of the Banat and Batchka. people who are now settled all over the world from Alaska, America, Austria, Australia, Canada, China, England, France, Germany, Ireland, New Zealand, The Philippines, Scotland, South America, Turkey, even Japan. They all express their extreme gratitude to me for publishing these recipes on the Internet. All grew up with these recipes in happier times, and for one reason or another, the recipes died out with the death of a grandmother or mother. Rare was the family who had all the recipes preserved on paper. "What was once lost, is now found" is the general refrain of the letters. All correspondents identify personally with the little stories that precede each recipe. Food preparation is a universal family theme. Memories of a family preparing their ancestral foods together arouse sentimental feelings for a distant heritage.

I call them Authentic Heirloom Recipes because they have survived in our family for many generations intact, not bastardized by modern convenience ingredients, or ingredients that were not available in Hungary over the last 200 years.

The authenticity of these recipe has been well received by modern day Hungarians. Since January 1997 these recipes have been featured and published one recipe a week by a Budapest electronic newspaper, "The Hungary Report". I regularly receive fan mail from the newspaper subscribers who are delighted to have these recipes. They swear they are just like their grandparents recipes.

**Danube Swabian
Coat of Arms**

Table of Contents

Introduction

Recipe Category Index

Authentic Hungarian Recipes

Relish & Pickles

Salads & Slaws

Soups and Dumplings

Main course

Side dishes

Sauces

Pastries

The Origin of June Meyer's Family Recipes

June Violet Wischler-Meyer is a retired public school Art teacher who taught at Wilmot Elementary School in Deerfield Illinois for 24 years. She is a graduate of the School of the Art Institute of Chicago. B.A.E. 1958.

I was born in Chicago in 1934. My Mother, Theresa Rose Sehne, my Father, Frank John Wischler and my Grandmother, Elizabeth Rose Heinz, cooked Hungarian and Transylvania dishes. The recipes I have posted as "Authentic Heirloom Hungarian Recipes" are just that. The recipes are descended from a long line of my ancestors, passed down from one generation to the next. They were never written down. I learned to make them by example. When I married, I continued to cook the cuisine I knew and loved. I love to cook, and I enjoy cooking and eating many different ethnic foods. But there is something spiritual and comforting about cooking and baking foods that your ancestors loved and thrived on. A lot of these recipes have their origin in Austria-Hungary. They are peasant dishes which took advantage of the bounty of the land, requiring slow cooking while the farmers worked in the fields. These are stick to the ribs, clog your arteries food. But they are exceptionally flavorful and unforgettable.

I do not carry Hungarian blood, but I like to think I do, because of the strong bond formed by a lifetime of cooking and eating Hungarian foods. The first lullaby I heard as a baby was a Hungarian one. The dance I loved was a Hungarian one. I used to think that my ancestral heritage was Hungarian because we cooked, baked and ate only Hungarian foods. All our family friends were from Hungary but we were all German speaking!

My father was born in Glockovatz, Translyvania. He used to tell me when I was little that his ancestors were glassmakers from the Black Forest in Germany. I found out through research that in the early 1700's many Germans from the Black Forest region emigrated to Translyvania, the Banat region, now part of Romania. They took advantage of a large give away of tracts of farmland. No taxes for 3 years, materials to build houses and farm buildings, some animal and beasts of burden, made these land giveaways popular.

These people were Catholics. They traveled to Ulm, Germany and then to Hungary via the Danube River on flat bottom barges. Today these settlers are known as Donau-Schwabins.

My Mother was born in Altkeer, Austria-Hungary, Batchka region. She always spoke of a maternal ancestor who was French and came from Alsace-Lorraine. I learned that Lutherans from Alsace-Lorraine were also offered land in Hungary, now Yugoslavia, around the mid 1700's. This information solved the puzzle of my German and French ancestry and Hungarian heritage.

My Mother and Father knew they were not Hungarians. But through the recesses of a hundred years or two, people no longer knew how they came to Hungary. They only knew things Hungarian. It had been their home for many generations. They knew no one in Germany or France. They remembered only fragments of information, shrouded by time. The two clues I had to help me reveal my ancestral past were, Black Forest and Alsace-Lorraine.

The political scene in that part of the world has been unstable since before WWI and most of the descendants of those German settlers left Hungary as Displaced Persons for America, Canada and Australia, and other parts of the world from the early 1900's to the mid 1950's.

If you are interested in learning more about these historical events, read Sue Clarkson's "History of German Settlement in Southern Hungary", (see page 171-186).

A Short Heinz-Sehne-Wischler Family History
1880 thru 1997

My parents, Theresa Rose Sehne and Frank John Wischler were both born in Austria-Hungary in the year 1905.

My mother's birthplace, Altkeer, Batchka is now part of Yugoslavia. Altkeer means "Old Gate". The ancient town was established in 1267.

The Sehne family owned and operated a Seltzer water bottling business that catered to a large clientele in town. My mother told stories of how she used to drive the team of horses when delivering the bottles of seltzer. Once the horses bolted and a few of the bottles blew up and cut her face. She had a scar across her nose for the rest of her life.

The Sehnes lived in a sturdy stone house that was surrounded by a wooden fence enclosing gardens for some vegetables, fruit trees and flower garden. The house had stone tile floors. The kitchen had two brick ovens built into the wall. I mention this because a lot of the houses had dirt floors and an oven in the yard. The Sehne's property was larger than most. It had to accommodate the Seltzer Works and a stable for the horses and delivery wagons. All the houses in their neighborhood fronted on a wide road which also served as a path for the cows to go the communal pastures. A village herdsman collected all the cows in the morning after their milking and returned them again for the evening milking. Each cow knew their home and would wait at the gate upon returning home, waiting for someone in the family to open the gate and admit her.

The whole Sehne family worked in the fields surrounding their village raising their food. The family was very self sufficient.They raised all the food they consumed. They grew wheat, potatoes, onions, garlic, summer squash and winter squash. Many kinds of beans, green and for drying. Peppers and chilies for Paprika sweet and hot, red, yellow and green varieties. Tomatoes red, heavy heart shaped. All kinds of roots: parsley, parsnip, carrots, turnips, beets, potatoes, white and sweet. They raised celery, cauliflower and cabbage for sour kraut. Pumpkins were grown large enough for a child to hide in, It was fed to man and beast. Alfalfa and field corn were grown to feed the animals. Huge leaves of Swiss chard with bright red veins were raised instead of the lesser yielding spinach. Many pickles and large plants of Dill weed were grown to use in canning.

Every homestead had fruit trees: apples, cherry, apricots, plums, pear, and peach. Lemons came from Italy. They raised melons of all kinds. There were many nut trees, walnut, filbert. Almonds came from the Middle East. Opium Poppies were an important crop to supply the poppy seeds for the Hungarian Mauk or Poppy Seed Strudel. The juice of the opium poppy was also important as a medicinal drink for sick people.

They planted bushes of currents, blackberries, raspberries, gooseberries and plants of strawberries. Grapes were grown to supply a store of home made wine and vinegar for the winter. Dried grapes became raisins for winter strudels.
They butchered their own pigs in late fall when the weather was cold, and smoked the hams, sausages and bacon. Cows were milked to make butter and sour cream and cheese. They raised chickens and geese whose down and feathers provided all the pillows and feather beds a family needed. My Grandmother carried her down featherbed to America. We spent many a winter sleeping under it. It supplied warmth for four generations.

Silk worms were also raised on the homestead. My mother told me stories of how she would collect mulberry leaves in large quantities to feed the silk worms they raised as an additional money crop. Sugar beet was another important money crop. They needed cash to buy sugar, coffee, chocolate for baking, to pay taxes, and many other necessary things.

The family also raised flax and prepared the flax in the streams and spun it into yarn for the looms to weave into linen bedding and clothes. A traveling itinerant weaver was hired to draft the patterns for the loom. The family would weave all winter long, as they were not needed in the fields. The linen was made into many articles to meet the needs of the house. When the linen sheets were laundered they were draped over bushes to dry in the sun. The sun would bleach the tan sheets into white over a number of years. Old sheets would become soft and white with use. They were then cut up for baby clothes, underwear, dish towels and petticoats.

Laundry soap was made out of the drippings of meats, and lard. It was cooked with lye that was made from wood ash. The soap was a strong soap, brown in color, and when cooked with the clothes got out the toughest stains. I remember my Mother making this soap in large wooden forms in our kitchen in Chicago.

Every villager wore an outfit that was unique to their village. The women and girls wore long full skirts with several petticoats underneath. The tops were a smock like blouse, high collared, long sleeves with ruffles over the shoulder, along the bust line and along the flared bottom hem. It was buttoned up the back and was usually of a patterned material of cotton or linen. A long apron would be tied around the waist. Every villager had a "good" outfit to wear to church or for special occasions. It would include a fancy shawl to wear about the shoulder, and festive ribbons and decoration for the hair depending on how old you were.

Leather shoes and boots were very precious. Shoes were expensive and most people would have one pair last them for many years. Children's leather shoes were always handed down in the family.

Every one, including men, wore in the house hand knitted or crocheted slippers made of tight wool with soft leather soles sewn on the bottom. All the old grandmothers could be seen knitting these slippers. They fit your foot tightly, some had a strap and button across the instep, some had none. They all had a toe that came to a point. These could be worn at home, on the road, or in the wooden shoes for the field. They wore out and you had to keep replacing them. I remember my Grandmother Sehne and my Mother knitting these slippers. As a child, I took it for granted that everyone in Chicago wore these.

This was an extended family. Besides my mother Theresa Rose and her sister Elizabeth Sofia, her older married sister Barbara Simon and her Husband, there were also her widowed mother Elizabeth Rose and her Grandmother Sehne. There were also two sisters of father Johann. Aunt Sofia Sehne, who would later marry into the Johann Donner family, and Aunt Barbara Sehne who would marry John Miller, a widower with one son whose name was John. Aunt Barbara never bore children of her own.

My mother's father, Johann died of war wound complications in 1909 when she was only 4.

Because of the political unrest in Eastern Europe, My Grandmother Sehne went to American to visit a cousin, Julianna Sehne in Cleveland Ohio, who wrote glowing reports of life in the new world. Before she could return to Europe, World War One started and she had to remain here until the war was over. Her two young daughters, Theresa, my Mother and, Elizabeth my Aunt were left in the care of her sister-in-law Aunt Sofia Sehne Donner for the duration of the war. Grandmother returned to Europe on the very first boat that sailed from New York to Europe.

After the war, their land and homes were given over to Serbia and Yugoslavia. Austria Hungary was carved up and the ethnic Germans were persuaded to leave.

Grandma Sehne's oldest daughter Barbara was married by this time and she decided to stay with her husband. She died several years later.

Grandmother Sehne left for America this time with her two daughters, Theresa and Elizabeth. Her Aunt Barbara Sehne Miller and her husband John Miller and his son John were already settled in Chicago waited for them to come to America.

My Mother (as did her sister, my Aunt Betty) started working for the Phoenix Trimming Company in Chicago on Racine Street and Armitage, when she first came to America. Phoenix manufactured silk tassels for lamps and draperies, gimp and trimmings for clothes and furniture. They also made wonderful all cotton throw rugs in assorted colors and patterns. She started out as a teenage spool girl and worked her way up to become a Fore lady and Supervisor. She won awards for her fine government work during W.W.II when Phoenix made parachute straps for our armed forces and later Auto safety belts. She worked there until her retirement at 65!

My father Frank John Wischler was born in Transylvania in a town called Glockovatz, Banat region. It is in the Carpathian Mountains. After World War I it became part of Romania. My grandfather Wendel or Willard Wischler was a vintner in Transylvania as was his father before him. He had tracts of vineyards.

An unknown reason caused the decision to leave the Banat in 1910. Perhaps it was because of mandatory Army servitude. At any rate, My Grandfather Wendel and his 16 year old son Andrew Wischler by a deceased wife, his four young children born to a second wife, Anna Leonard, left Glockovatz for America. My uncle Andrew was the oldest. He would marry Raginna in America. Wendel was 10 or 12? Next came Michael age 8, my father Frank John age 5 and finally little Kate age 3. They chose Chicago to come to because an Aunt and Uncle John Wischler lived on Orchard Street and would help them get settled.

A few years after arrival from Transylvania, Grandfather Wendel Wischler wanted the family to return to his vineyards. Grandmother Anna Wischler refused to go back to the old world. Grandfather left his family for Glockovatz, never to see them all again. They received a letter that he had died after many years.

Life was hard for the immigrant Wischler family in Chicago. But they had the "German work ethic" and knew what hard work was and they all helped to earn a living.

My father, Frank John Sr. as a little boy sold newspapers on the street. He said he carried a brick in the bottom of a burlap bag and would swing it around his head to keep the ruffian kids from stealing the money he earned until he got home. He was 7.

Home was at 1916 N. Burling Street in what is now called a "Historic Cottage". It was built right after the Great Chicago Fire of 1871. It originally was built as a two flat, each with two bedrooms, kitchen, toilet, dinning room and parlor. Years before my Grandmother Wischler bought the house, it had been altered to become a three flat with the upstairs flat converted to two flats each with one or two small bedrooms, kitchen, living room and a shared common bath.

St. Michael's Church was the parish church and school that my father went to. Grandmother took in young boarder to make ends meet. The boarders were friends of my father and uncles. They were all immigrants from the Banat in Transylvania. Some were from the same town. Their names were Michael Graef, Philip Rothschiller, Frank Zellner. They became life long family friends.

The neighborhood was an old one, filled with Catholic immigrant families mainly from Germany and

Hungary, with some from Italy and Ireland. The various ethnic groups did not intermingle easily. The Italians associated with the Italians. The Irish associated with the Irish. It was not until the first born generation went to public schools that various ethnic and religious groups began to associate and befriend one another.
The Germans and Hungarians prided themselves on their work ethic and their clean houses. (I thought everyone did a major Spring cleaning with all the walls and ceilings being washed down, the rugs taken out and beaten with wire rug beaters, kitchen cupboards and all china and glass ware washed and polished and all curtains taken down, washed and stretched on wooden frames with short needles to dry). My mother would always remark that "soap is cheap, there is no excuse for being dirty. We may be poor, but we take pride in cleanliness".

My father as a teenager worked in the Chicago Stockyards for a time. Family lore has it that his mother made him change his clothes out in the hallway of the flat because he smelled so bad when he came home from work. It was not common in those days to have a bath in every home. The family would go to the public baths to bath in hot water after a hard day of work. The laundry would be cooked in a large copper kettle (all homes did not have hot water heaters) on the stove and washed with home made soap on a wash board. In winter the wet wash was carried up some ladders to the attic where it would be hung to dry. Fat drippings were always collected to make soap with.

When my father was 16 he ran away from home to see "The West". He went to Nebraska to work on a ranch wrangling steer as he had done in the Chicago Stock Yards. There is a photo of him wearing cowboy gear, chaps, boots, vest, hat and scarf. It was taken before he was bucked by a bronco and was thrown into barbed wire. He too had a nice scar across his nose. He was called back home to attend the funeral of his favorite brother Michael, who died of a burst appendix at age 18 or 19.

Funeral were held in homes in those days. The family would make room for the open casket and it's bier in the living room or "Front Room" as they were then called. A photographer would make a "Memorial" photo of the family and friends posing with the open casket. It might be the only photo of the deceased the family has. We have only two photos of Michael. One taken as a child and one taken in death. Family and friends would come to pay their respects. Usually an envelope with some money would be handed to the bereaved to help pay for burial expenses. After the burial, friends and family would sit down to a large dinner, and divert one another with happy memories.

Burial plots were often leased for a period of time if you were poor, usually for 25 or 50 years after which the plot was emptied and used again. Graves of my Grandmother Wischler and her son Michael were for a specific time. They do not exist today. My Maternal Grandmother Sehne died when the family was more affluent and her grave and stone still exist in the St. Lucas Cemetary along with both my parents, Aunt Elizabeth, and Great Aunt Miller's graves.

I do not remember my grandmother Wischler. I was one or two when she died. I do have snatches of slight memories of a woman who wore a black scarf on her head, hiding her hair in the way Muslim women do. I also remember a lady with long skirts and many petticoats. My sister Theresa Elizabeth assures me she loved me very much. I am told she was always kissing me and my older brother Frank who hated to be kissed by anyone. He complained that when she kissed him while he was eating his meal, she spit in his food. Our father constructed a cardboard wall for him to use to protect his food from contamination. He would sit hidden behind this wall at the table. Eventually he put the cardboard screen away.

Grandmother Anna Wischler died in 1935 or 1936 in Chicago. She died on a frigid day in winter.

My parents met at a Glockovatz Kirchweg in 1924. A church fest held to commemorate the establishment of the catholic church in Glockovatz, Transylvania. Every year on the same date, all the Chicago people who originally came from the same town in Hungary would get together to dance, sing, and meet young people, possibly with marriage in mind.

My mother must have gone with a girl friend, because she was not Catholic and her Lutheran Church did not have dances. She met my father and against the wishes of my catholic Grandmother Wischler who prefered a Catholic girl, they were married the following year.

After my father was married he started to work for the Chicago Surface Lines, (later to become the Chicago Transit Authority). He retired after 40 years with the CTA. He started out as a Motorman on the old red streetcars and years later drove the new buses. He worked a split shift. He would go to work at five in the morning, return home around eleven and then go back again at one and be home around four for dinner time.

I would often take a hot Sunday lunch to my father by riding the Armitage streetcar to his depot at Cortland, visit while he ate, and then ride with him on his streetcar. I would sit on a seat at the front of the car to his left, and once in a while he would let me stomp on the floor bell. I loved the sway of the streetcars. I must have been 10 years old.

My father was seen in the kitchen as often as my mother. He often whistled when he started the preparation of the dinner meal. When my mother came home from work around 3:30 she would finish cooking the supper meal. All the recipes in this book were the recipes that we cooked every day, day after day. I did not realize then, what a precious culinary heritage was being left to me. I am forever grateful.

Most of my culinary memories as a child, center around the kitchen and the foods and baked goods we made for all festivities, such as Easter, Christmas, Birthdays, family celebrations, and Thanksgiving.

My Mother and Father were truly people of the land. When they were financially able, they purchased land in Lake George, Wisconsin. The property was about 50 miles north of Chicago. My father, who had only a third grade education, designed a house by cutting up cardboard boxes. He was not an educated man, but he was very intelligent and creative. In 1950 he not only drew his own building plans, but supervised the foundation digging and concrete pouring, and did all his own electrical, plumbing and heating work. With the help of my mother, and their friends, they raised all the framing of the walls. My mother and father built everything. Windows, floors, doors, kitchen cabinets, stairs. The house was a ranch, Two large bedrooms, a living-dining room combination, a large kitchen, large bath, an enclosed porch overlooking the gardens and an attic that supplied extra sleeping space. In the basement was a large room that held all the rows of home canned produce.

The first building to be erected on the land was an out house toilet and a shed to store the building tools between work periods as the house would be constructed on vacations and weekends over a two years span.

The second building constructed was a garage, that would serve as our weekend home during the time we all worked on the main house. It was one large room, built on a concrete slab. It had several windows, a door and a garage door. The first weekend it was used overnight, we lived like Gypsies. (No offense to Gypsies). There was an old smoky wood burning stove in the middle to give some heat and make coffee. There were several old beds, a large table, and open shelves to store food stuff and dishes. An old dresser to hold bed linens and towels. We even made Hungarian Gypsy Bacon over the wood stove. Nothing ever tasted so good to us that night.

As a teenager I thought this an adventure. Many family friends and relations would come out for the weekends to help and we always had a large number of people to feed.

My parents saw the land at Lake George for the first time, when they went to visit our city neighbors, who had purchased small summer cottages. They were impressed with the rich black virgin Wisconsin soil. There were also a lot of Austrian-Hungarians who owned summer cottages. The Bolenbachs, the Blums, the Kuechls, the Binders, all were our neighbors in Chicago on Burling Street.

My parents loved their weekend home in Wisconsin. They loved the land, and worked hard in the garden to produce wonderful things. Every thing grew amazingly large and bountiful those first years in the rich black virgin soil.

They knew how to compost and made use of it to enrich the soil. Many variety of vegetables were raised. What was not consumed or given away to family and friends was canned or frozen for use through the rest of the year. Fruits were made into jellies and jams, grapes were pressed and made into wine in wooden casks. Cabbage was cut and made into sauerkraut in large stoneware crocks, peppers and pickles were pickled in brine and bottled. Canning season was a lot of work, but I still remember the pride they had when they posed in front of their winters supply of canned food. Canned tomatoes, peaches, plums, pears, apples, cherries, zucchini winter squash with dill, beets, I must be forgetting something! They froze large packets of green beans, bell peppers, sweet corn, broccoli, carrots, soup greens, parsley, and dill.

They smoked meat, ham, bacon and home made Hungarian sausages in the back yard of our small house in Chicago.

My Mother loved flowers and her garden in the country produced many bouquets. We always had fresh flowers in the house from spring to late fall.

My mother saw to it that we children went to Sunday School and made our confirmations in the Lutheran Church.

My father was catholic but never attended church except on Christmas or Easter when he accompanied my mother to her lutheran church, St. James on Fremont Street in Chicago.

He was a just man, who worked hard to support not only his growing family, but his mother, mother-in-law and at times his wife's sister and her son. He was industrious, loyal to his wife, loved his children, never drank to excess. He loved to cook, eat, dance and make love (I'm sure). He knew how to do everything. He could repair anything around the house, electric, plumbing, gas water heaters, oil stoves. He could finish concrete, lay bricks, do carpentry work, plow and plant a garden, hang wallpaper, lay wooden floors, build furniture, glaze windows, build a house. I never saw him lazy.

On a beautiful fall day my father died of a massive coronary occlusion one month after he retired, from his long years of work, at age 65. He had been whistling all morning, helping my mother with the dishes and was sitting in a lawn chair under a tree in Wisconsin when he quietly died.

My mother was also a hardworking woman. She provided us with the same work ethic she was raised with. She believed that the morning hours were "golden". She got up early at five in the morning, made breakfast for us while we were still sleeping, made her bed, took her bath and left for work at the factory hours before we children would get up to go to school. Even after her retirement she continued to arise early.

She took her commitment to her family very seriously. She instilled in us a respect for hard work. We children all helped around the house. She taught us how to "Make Order" in the house. We cleaned the house, crawling around the floor to polish the legs of the tables and chairs with banana smelling polish. We crawled under the beds to dust the bed springs.

No dust bunnies here. We washed floors on our knees to get into the corners, we helped wash the windows with Bon-Ami, swept the floors with straw brooms. She taught us how to avoid getting our fingers caught in the rollers of the old washing machine. We learned to wipe the clothes line with a cloth before hanging up the wash with wooden clothes pins, how to iron clothes by sprinkling water out of a wine bottle with a metal sprinkle top. We learned to appreciate the wonderful scent of sun and air on bed linens after a windy day on the line. She taught us to cook the dishes she was taught to cook and she was proud of our accomplishments. Family ties were important to her. We had a close knit family, with countless Uncles, Aunts, Great aunts, Grandmothers, cousins, sisters, brothers and in-laws.

My Mother loved gardening. She thought it a sin against God, not to use the bounty of the land. If we had crab apple trees (which we did) we made jars of crab apple jelly. We had grapes, we made wine and jelly. She saved her own seeds from year to year, and successfully raised new generations of vegetable and flowers. She shared seeds and cuttings with friends. She grew large sun flowers for the birds and squirrels. She planted shrubs with berries friendly to the birds.

My mother loved music. She loved all the Strauss waltzes and German Operettas. She loved dancing. European custom allows women to dance not only with men but with other women. At family weddings and Kirchwegs I learned to dance polkas and waltzes by dancing with my mother, and by standing on the toes of my father's shoes.

My Mother died of breast cancer in 1977 at age 72.

Our parents taught us to love and respect ourselves and others, to honor our heritage, and to try to live productive and caring lives. I think we have all tried.

A Word About Hungarian Christmas Cookies

A month and a half before Christmas my Mother would start baking many cookies to see us thru the Holiday Season. Hungarian cookies usually are made from butter or lard, dried fruits, nuts of all kinds, sour cream, cream cheese, spices and lemon zest. Very old recipes usually do not contain baking powder, but rely on lots of eggs. It was common for a cookie recipe to call for 24 egg yolks.

As a child, I remember the whole family sitting around the kitchen table, picking the nut meats out of the walnuts, hazelnuts, pecans, and almonds. We would pound the nuts open with a hammer and use the nut picks to pick out the meat. One for the bowl, one for the mouth. My Mother would yell at us to not eat so many, she needed them for the cookies. My Grandmother sat at the table with the nut mill she brought from Hungary and milled the nuts for the cookies and strudels. Other nuts were chopped for sprinkling on top of cookies. It was a wonderful day when nut companies started selling shelled nuts in the store. Something was gained but something was also lost.

Some cookies were rolled out and cut with the old cookies cutters from Hungary, some were pressed into an ancient copper cookie mold in the shape of a bundle of wheat and gently knocked out. Other cookies were rolled in the hand and baked and then rolled in powdered sugar or sugar and milled nuts.

Pounds of dried Apricots and dried Prunes were cooked on the stove with water and sugar to make the Lekvar for Kipfils and cookies. No store bought Apricot or Prune filling can compare with the home made. Lekvar will keep for a year in a covered jar in the refrigerator, longer in the freezer.

The cookie most beloved and treasured was the Linzerteig (dough from Linz, Austria). It meant that we children would be helping to cut the cookies out and decorating them.

The old cookie cutters were large and small. Hand made and soldered more than 150 years ago, the cutters were black with many years of use.

Hearts, Diamonds, Spades, Clubs, Crescent Moons, Stars, Suns. No Frosty the Snowman, or Rudolph, no Christmas trees, no Angels. Just the celestial bodies and the suits of cards. I have an uncomfortable suspicion that these cookie cutter symbols are more pagan than Christian.

After the cookies were cut from the dough, we would coat the top of the raw cookie with some egg white that was beaten with a few drops of water, and then sprinkle some decorations on it. Colored sugars, mixtures of chopped nuts and sugar, half of a candied cherry or a dab of Lekvar.

Baking would go on for weeks. The washing of the Cookie pans was my job. It was a never ending job. The wet dish towels hung over the oven to dry. Pans going into the oven and pans coming out of the oven. Cookies burn very quickly if they are not watched. You can alway tell by smell when the cookies are done. There is a fine line between "done" and "burned". This was serious business!

At least 20 different cookies and three kinds of Strudels, Walnut, Poppy Seed and Raisin would be made. Trays of Kipfels with assorted fillings, Prune, Apricot, nut, and cheese would be made before the baking was finally done. All of the family cooking pots, roasters, and cookie tins were filled with cookies. We had a stairway leading up to an unheated attic. Every step held two pots, or roasters. The cookies would keep fresh till they were made into gift platters for our neighbors, friends, and co-workers.

My mother never forgot anyone. All received a generous platter of Hungarian Cookies, Kipfels, and Strudels for Christmas. She was much appreciated for her loving labors. This was the way it was done in the old days. She continued this practice all her life, until her 70's when she died.

My sister, Theresa Jerger of Kalispell, Montana, and I inherited not only the cookie recipes, but all the cookie sheets, strudel pans and cookie cutters, molds and the willingness to continue this Christmas Cookie tradition, but on a more limited scale.

A Word About Ingredients Used In June Meyer's Authentic Hungarian Recipes

•**Paprika**, Hungarians use an amazing amount of Paprika. If you are going to make Hungarian dishes you must buy imported Paprika. Do not use the paprika in the little jars in the supermarket. It is not the same quality as imported. Paprika comes in six categories: exquisite delicate, delicate, noble sweet, semi-sweet, rose, and hot. I usually buy Szeged brand Paprika "Sweet Delicacy". It is not spicy but has excellent flavor. If you want fiery hot, then look for paprika labeled "Eros" which means hot. Any Paprika labeled "Sweet" or "Edesmes" has a lack of spiciness.

•**Lard and butter**, Many of these recipes call for lard. If it is a pastry do not omit lard. It gives the dough a flakiness and crispness characteristic of a lot of Hungarian pastry. If a recipe calls for butter, use butter. Do not use margarine. It will not give the best results and flavor. In frying recipes such as doughnuts, Listys etc. Lard can stand a much higher temperature than Oil, but never let it get so hot that it smokes.

•**Eggs**, If a recipe calls 24 egg yolks, use 24 egg yolks, not 12 whole eggs. It will not work.

•**Oil**, Some recipes such as coleslaw, cucumber salad call for oil. I like to use corn oil or peanut oil rather than olive oil which is too heavy and flavored.

•**Vinegar**, Hungarians use a lot of vinegar in their foods. Pickled hot peppers, Dill Pickles, Coleslaws, Cucumber Salads, Tomato Salads, Potato Salads, Potato Soup, all Bean soups, Lentil soup, sauces such as Dill, Tomato, Calf Liver with Onions and some pastry doughs all contain vinegar. Most Hungarian dishes lend themselves to white vinegar rather than red. Red vinegar will muddy the color of dishes made with sour cream. You can use a good white wine vinegar or cider vinegar. I use a Japanese rice wine vinegar. It is delicate and does not compete with the flavor of slaws, cucumbers, sour creams etc.

•**Sugar**, You will notice that Hungarians love to cook with sugar. The Hungarians have known for generations that a little sugar makes food taste wonderful. You will find a teaspoon or tablespoon of sugar in Coleslaw, Cucumber Salads, Sauerkraut, Tomato Soup, Szekely Gulyas, Potato Salad, Tomato Sauce, Dill Sauce and Sour Cream with Horseradish Sauce, Smoked Butt, and Cabbage Soup and Onion Gravy and Zucchini Squash with Dill.

•**Apricots and Prunes**, Hungarian pastries always call for "Lekvar" which is pure puree of Apricot or Prune cooked with sugar. No fillers, preservatives, artificial color. This is the preferred filling for cookies and Kipfels. It is easy to make, so do not buy the canned filling. Lekvar is full of flavor, and a pound of dried fruit will make a large amount that can be kept in the freezer.

•**Poppy Seeds**, If you are going to make Poppy Seed Strudel or Moon Strudel, you will have to find an Imported Food store to get your fresh ground poppy seed by the pound. Do not buy the little sprinkle bottles in the spice section of the supper market. These are too little, too expensive and not fresh enough. Ask the Imported Store salesperson to grind the seeds twice for you. If they cannot grind the seeds for you, you can grind them yourself in an electric coffee bean grinder. The ground seeds should look like finely ground black pepper with little particles of black, white and grey visible. Nothing is worse than poppy seed filling in a strudel that is not ground well. It has a very disturbing "mouth feel", and has no proper flavor.

•**Sour Cream**, Do not use imitation or low fat sour cream if you want your Hungarian dish to taste authentic. Hungarians use a lot of sour cream in their everyday dishes and pastries. A lot of pastry recipes call for some sour cream. Sour cream is usually added to Gulyas and Paprikas at the end of the cooking process. Sour cream is used as a topping on Palacintas, Plum Dumplings, crepes, as well as on Cabbage casseroles, Potato Soup, Cabbage Soup, Tomato Soup.It is also an important ingredient in Sour Cherry Soup and Dill Squash. If you must watch calories, lessen the amount.

•**Lemon**, If a recipe calls for lemon zest or lemon juice do not substitute dried zest or juice in a bottle or plastic lemon. In old Hungarian Strudel, or pastry recipes, you will never find vanilla or other extracts listed in the ingredients. The grated zest of lemon was usually used to flavor the dough. Often a recipe will call for the zest and the juice of the lemon to flavor the dough.

•**Nuts**, Walnuts and Hazelnuts were the traditional nuts used in Hungarian pastries. Nusse Strudel would not be right if made with anything but ground walnuts.

•**Flour**, The dumpling, pastry and strudel recipes call for all purpose flour. Do not use cake flour unless specified.

•**Bacon**, A lot of Hungarian recipes call for some bacon. Hungarian bacon is smoked, covered in Paprika and full of intense flavor. It is usually sold unsliced with the rind attached. It is also very expensive and found only in imported food shops and some specialty butcher shops. You can substitute any good thick cut smoked bacon and get good results.

•**Sauerkraut**, Hungarians make and eat a lot of sauerkraut. In todays modern world, excellent sauerkraut can be purchased in most stores. I prefer buying kraut in bottles or in plastic pouches. Canned kraut often has a metallic taste. The kraut should look fresh, that is, it should be white or off white, never brown or tan. If you like really sour sauerkraut, use with out rinsing in water. I like to rinse my sauerkraut under cold running water and drain before using. If you want creamy kraut, when it is cooking, add a large raw grated potato to the kraut about 1/2 hour before it is done and tender. It will make it silky and creamy.

•**Cabbage**, Cabbage was an important food crop in Hungary. It grew large and stored well. The Hungarians devised many recipes using fresh cabbage. It was never just boiled in water, but rather sauteed in butter or bacon fat, mixed with meat or vegetables or fruit, covered in sour cream or tomatoes. It can have an amazingly delicate and nutty flavor. There is even a Cabbage Strudel.

•**Tomatoes**, Tomato is an important ingredient in Hungarian cooking. When you cook dishes that call for tomatoes, you can use canned ones instead of fresh. Most of us cannot get good homegrown tomatoes and it is preferred to use good canned ones instead of the tastless ones from the SUPER MARKET. I use canned crushed tomatoes for Tomato Soup, Tomato Sauce, Szekely Gulyas. Hungarian Chicken

Soup alway has a small whole unpeeled tomato in it to give the soup a "blush". Note: Hungarian Stuffed Cabbage or Sorma NEVER has tomato in it, nor does authentic Hungarian Gulyas.

•**Spices and Herbs**, Hungarians cook with many spices and Herbs that give their dishes subtle but intricate flavors.

•**Dill**, Always use fresh dill or fresh dill that you have frozen for recipes calling for dill. Do not use dried dill. You will not get any flavor.

•**Bay Leaf**, Two or three are used in Potato Soup. Do not omit. I also use bay leaves in Szeged Gulyas, Stuffed Green Pepper, Sorma, sauerkraut.

•**Whole Clove**, Two or three whole cloves are always stuck into a whole onion for Beef Soup and Chicken Soup. Two or three whole cloves are always included in Lentil Soup, Smoked Butt, Cabbage Soup and Split Pea Soup.

•**Peppercorns**, A few whole black peppercorns are added to all soups, sauerkraut, Stuffed Green pepper.

•**Mace**, An important spice for Chicken Soup and other chicken dishes.

•**Caraway seed**, Some sauerkraut dishes will call for caraway seed. It is important in Roast Pork with Sauerkraut and Onion Gravy dish. Do not omit in this dish.

•**Dill seed**, Several heads of dried dill seed and dried dill stalk is necessary for the dill flavor of Dill Sun Pickles. Do not omit. Do not use very fresh dill for pickling. Wilted is fine.

•**Parsley leaf**, When a recipe calls for chopped parsley, use the fresh Italian flat leaf parsley. It has a finer flavor. I chop the parsley leaves in my Cuisinart and store in a jar in the freezer. The Parsley Poultry Stuffing uses several cups of parsley. Never subsitute dry for fresh.

•**Parsley root**, An indespensible ingredient in any Hungarian Split Pea Soup, Beef or Chicken Soup. Use the cleaned parsley root whole along with the attached parsley leaves.

•**Parsnip root**, Along with Parsley root, Parsnip root is indespensible for making a good Pea, Beef or Chicken Soup. Parsnip can be a little woody so use the root whole for its flavor.

•**Garlic**, If garlic is called for please use fresh garlic not the minced kind in a jar. Garlic is cheap and the flavor is better if it is minced just before you use it.

•**Celery**, Celery is always used ribs whole in Beef Soup and Chicken Soup. It is alway chopped or sliced for Bean soup, Pea Soup and Lentil Soup. Slice thinly for Potato Salads and Tomato Salads.

•**All spice**, The main flavor in Hungarian Sausage along with garlic and paprika.

•**Onions**, I prefer unpeeled yellow onions for Beef and Chicken Soup because the peel imparts nice gold color to the soup. White or yellow onions can be used for most recipes requiring chopped onions.

•**Hungarian Sausage**, You can usually find a butcher shop that specializes in German or Hungarian sausages. They usually make a Hungarian fresh and smoked sausage. Hungarian Sausage is made from pork shoulder, paprika, garlic, allspice, salt and pepper. Fresh Hungarian Sausage is cooked in water first, and then fried when the water has evaporated. It becomes a Mahogany color from all the paprika.

•**Smoked Hungarian Sausage**, Fresh sausage is slowly smoked until most of the moisture is removed. Smoked sausage is always more expensive per pound than fresh because so much weight is lost in smoking. It is used in Potato Soup, Sauerkraut dishes, Bean Soups, Cabbage dishes, Sauerkraut, where ever a good smokey flavor is wanted. A little goes a long way.

•**Potatoes**, I think the best potato for Hungarian dishes is the Red or New Potato. It holds together well in Gulyas and Potato Soups, it mashes well for potato dumpling dough.

June Meyer's Authentic Hungarian Heirloom Recipes

Category Index

Authentic Hungarian Cucumber Relish from Tante Betty

I can't be too sure that this recipe is an old recipe since it relies on refrigeration to keep it for 3 or 4 months. But I do know that we used this recipe at the end of summer when the cucumbers were plentiful and we stocked our crock for a winter of relish.

- 6 to 7 peeled cucumbers, thin sliced
- 1 large onions, thin sliced
- 1 Tablespoon of salt

Mix all in a bowl and let sit for 3 hours. After 3 hours, pour off excess liquid. Add 2 cups of sugar and 1 cup of white vinegar. Mix and store in covered glass jar or dish in refrigerator. Will keep up to 3 or 4 months.

Authentic Hungarian Dill Sun Pickles

A family favorite are Dill pickles made in the summer sun. Nothing could be easier to make or tastier to eat. All that is needed is a secure place in the sunshine where your bottles of sun pickles can sit unmolested by little children who can't wait for the pickles to be sun cooked. The usual method was to collect the pickles every day fresh off of the vine. This way you could have a fresh bottle going every other day. We ate a lot of pickles. It takes a few days for the pickles to cook. After they are done, the bottle is stored in the refridgerator. Cold, crunchy, dilly. We kids would eat them like a pop-sickle. The envy of all the neighbor hood kids.

- Pickles, not cucumbers
- Hot boiling water
- Clean jars or bottles

Per each quart bottle

- 1 tsp. sugar
- 1 1/2 Tbls. salt
- 1 1/2 shot glass of vinegar, about 2 1/2 Tbls.
- 2 or 3 seed heads and stems of dill
- Boiling water to cover pickles

Wash pickles, trim ends and split the pickle down the middle with a knive so the brine can flow through. Pack pickles in clean jars or bottles. Place on top of pickles the sugar, salt, vinegar, and the dill weed. Pour boiling water over the pickles to cover. Shake to mix up the brine, and cover with a loose lid or plate and set bottle where the sun will shine on it for several hours a day.

At first the pickles will be bright green, but in one or two days days more or less depending on the amount of sun, the pickles will absorb the brine and have the usual pickle look. The brine will change also. When you remove a pickle always use a clean fork. Otherwise you will contaminate the brine and spoil the pickle. Never use your fingers unless you are going to finish the whole bottle in one orgy of pickle eating. Store in the refridgerator.

P.S. Take the pickle bottles in at night. Raccoons have been know to raid the bottle.

Authentic Hungarian Green Tomato Relish

Summer time was never a time of ease and leisure. The produce was ripening in the garden and that meant more canning to do. Relishes were always a welcome addition to the table during the winter. My parents never bought comercially prepared pickles, peppers, relishes. We alway made our own. The Green Tomato Relish would rid the garden of all the tomatoes that never wanted to ripen. It is a wonderful, tasty, spicy relish that will accent any meal. Great with sandwiches.

- 10 lbs. of green tomatoes
- 1 head of cauliflower or more
- 5 lbs. of peeled yellow or white onions
- 5 green bell peppers
- 5 red peppers
- 1 cup of pickling salt (no iodine)

Brine

- 7 cups of vinegar. White is best
- 1 whole box of mixed pickling spices
- 1 box of whole mustard seed
- 5 cups of sugar

Slice thinly only the tomatoes, onions and cauliflower. Place the cut up vegetables in a large plastic bin. Sprinkle 1 cup of salt over vegetables and let it sit over night. Drain well and rinse off salt with water. Remove the seeds from the red and green peppers and cut up into small pieces. Add the rinsed off vegetables and place in large kettle or pot along with the vinegar, mustard seeds. Place the mixed pickling spices in a bag or cloth to keep them together so they can be fished out later. Mustard seeds remain in the relish. Cook until vegetable are soft, not mushy! Remove mixed spice bag and add 5 cups of sugar. Cook ten more minutes until sugar is melted. Bottle in sterilized canning jars. Makes a lot!

Authentic Hungarian Cole Slaw (Kaposztsalata)

I find it amusing that in my kitchen, I have all the latest culinary gadgets, from coffee bean grinders, cusinarts, can openers, coffee makers, juicers, and so on, to aid me in my cooking adventures, yet when I want cole slaw I get out my hand held "Rapid Slaw Cutter" (cica 1950). Made by the Bluffton Slaw Cutter Co. Bluffton, Ohio. This non-technical hand held cutter sold for about 39 cents way back then. It cuts the cabbage into delicate strands of slaw. Better than any Cusinart can. If you frequent garage sales, or estate sales, you may be lucky enough to find a used one. Frequent use will keep it sharp. My cutter is willed to my son.

- 1 cabbage head
- 1/2 small onion
- good white vinegar
- oil, peanut or corn is fine
- sugar
- salt and pepper

Slice cabbage head into slaw. Place slaw into bowl. Mince 1/2 small onion and add to bowl. Add 2 Tbl. white vinegar. Add 5 Tbl. oil. Add 1 tsp. sugar, about 1/2 tsp. Salt. Wash hands and take off rings. Place your hands into the slaw, mix and squeeze the slaw so it makes some juice. This will make the slaw limp. Taste, add more salt if needed. Refrigerate till serving time. Good the next day also.

Serves 4 to 6.

Authentic Hungarian Cucumber Salad with Sour Cream (Tejfeles Uborkasalata)

This cucumber salad is by far one of the most delicious and refreshing salads you can eat. It has a wonderful cucumber flavor that is enhanced by the garlic and sour cream. Originally this was a summer salad to accompany roast meat or chicken dishes. Now that we have cucumbers available all year round we can enjoy this dish all year.

I use a slaw slicer to slice the cucumber thinly enough to see through! As a child I always enjoyed peeling and then grooving the cucumbers with the tines of a fork before my mother would slice them. I loved the refreshing cool cucumber spray that would mist my face.

- 4 cucumbers
- 1 small clove of garlic
- 1 teaspoon sugar
- 1/4 teaspoon salt
- 1/4 cup of good vinegar (not red)
- 3/4 cup of real sour cream

Peel cukes. Drag fork tines down length of peeled cucumbers to create long groves that will look very nice when you slice cucumbers very, very thin. Put in mixing bowl. Peel and chop clove of garlic. Add Salt and sugar slices. Mix in sour cream. Add vinegar (I like to use seasoned gourmet Rice Vinegar) and toss well, I use my hands, till cucumbers slices and sour cream are all frothy and foamy. Place in serving dish and sprinkle a little paprika on top for decoration, and serve well chilled. This will stay good in refridgerator for a few days.

Serves 4.

Authentic Hungarian Dill Potato Salad (Kapros krumplisalata)

Dill plants, green and feathery, tall and swaying in the breeze perfuming the air in the garden. Whole bunches of dill, three feet long or more hang drying in the summer kitchen waiting for the harvest canning to begin. Dill is still a staple in our household. Today, I buy bunches at the suppermarket and roll and wrap the fronds tightly in aluminum foil to store in my freezer for use all year round in salads, sauces, dips and soups.

This Dill Potato Salad Recipe is my favorite. It is full of fresh dill flavor. It is simple to make, embarass-ingly quick and mouthwatering.

- 6 red potatos
- 1/2 small onion
- 1 Tbls. minced fresh dill (do not subsitute dry)
- 3 Tbl. oil, corn or olive is fine
- 1 and 1/2 Tbl. of good white vinegar
- 1 tsp. sugar
- salt

Cook potatos in pot of salted water till tender. Cool enough to handle and peel. Slice potatos as for salad. Put potatos into a bowl. Add diced onion. Add minced fresh Dill. Pour oil and vinegar over ingredients in bowl. sprinkle 1 tsp. suger over all and toss to mix. Taste and adjust seasoning. More salt or more sugar if needed. Serve at room temperature.

Serves 4.

Authentic Hungarian Hot Bacon Potato Salad (Sultszalonnas krumplisalata)

Here is the Hungarian staple food, potatoes. Hungarian have made an art of using the potato. There is a summer Potato Salad with Sour Cream and Eggs, and a winter potato salad with hot bacon. My father was the one that made the dressing for this dish. He would roll up his sleeves, put on one of my mother's aprons and slice the bacon and fry it just right. This potato salad is best made fresh and served. Make the diners wait for the Hot Bacon Potato Salad. You do not want it to get cold. Serve warm.

- 8 whole red potatoes washed
- 1 small onion
- 1/4 lb. bacon
- 3 Tbl. vinegar
- 2 Tbs. flour
- 2 tsp. sugar
- 1 tsp. salt
- 1 cup water

Cook potatoes in boiling water until tender. Peel, cut into slices, not too small, and place in mixing bowl. Dice and fry in frying pan 1/4 lb. bacon, till almost crisp. Do not let burn. Remove diced bacon and place into mixing bowl with other ingredients. Peel and dice onion and place into reserved bacon fat. Saute a few minutes. Remove sauted diced onion with slotted spoon and place into mixing bowl. Into at least 2 Tbs. bacon fat, cook 2 Tbs. flour until smooth and bubbly, add 3 Tbs. vinegar and 2 teaspoon sugar, 1 tsp. salt, and enough water to make a medium sauce (about 1 cup or more). Bring to a boil and cook until sauce is thickened. Pour over ingredients in mixing bowl, and toss and mix. Taste, if needed add more salt. (Vinegar and Bacon are salty, so add salt last). Serve with hot baked ham, or sausage. Good with a hot bean dish or salad.
Salad serves 4.

Authentic Hungarian Hot Lettuce Salad with Bacon (Meleg salata szalonnaval)

We always ate some kind of salad with our suppers. Not a small plate with a few leaves of lettuce salad. This was a large bowl that was filled with all kinds of lettuce ready to be tossed with homemade salad dressing. We always used an oil and vinegar, or sour cream and vinegar based dressing. A store bought salad dressing would never be found in the house. In summer the salad greens would be heavy with sliced tomatoes, green onions and cucumbers. In summer vast quantities of thinly sliced cucumber salads with sour cream were consumed. Winter salads were usually thinly shredded cabbage slaws.

My father always kept a very small frying pan handy for his Hot Lettuce Salad with Bacon. This was a salad that kept us waiting. It had to be served right away. If you make it ahead of time all the greens will turn dark and limp. It was my father's job to get the salad dressing cooked and then mixed into the salad. I can still see him wearing my mother's apron, tied high under his arms to better protect his clothes from the spatters of bacon fat. This was a dish we often had, although as a child I never liked the curly endive. I could not manage to chew it. I still can not chew it.

Mixed salad greens, use endive, romaine, fresh spinach and leaf lettuce. Iceberg lettuce will wilt too fast and is not very flavorful.

- 1/3 cup of diced smoked Hungarian bacon
- 2 Tbls. vinegar
- 3 Tbls. water
- 1 tsp. sugar
- salt and pepper

In a frying pan sauté 1/3 cup of diced Hungarian smoked bacon or regular thick cut bacon.
After the bacon has rendered, remove the bacon dice, leaving the bacon fat.

In the bacon fat, stir in the vinegar, sugar and water. Let it come to a boil.
Replace the bacon dice and pour over the prepared greens. Add salt and pepper to taste and toss.
Serve immediately.

Will serve 2 or 4 depending on portion size.

Authentic Hungarian Style Tomato Salad (Paradicsomsalata)

This salad was always on the table during the summer months when the garden was producing. It requires fresh sun ripened tomatoes. We grew tomatoes of every decription. Big Boy, Little Boy, Big Girl, Beefsteak, Yellow no acid, Heinz, orange, cherry, Hungarian, Italian, names I can't remember. My father loved this salad. He would often add a tablespoon of water to the oil and vinegar to cut the acidity. When the salad bowl was empty of salad, we would skim off the countless seeds of tomato floating in the vinegar water and eat them. Believing that they contained special norishment.

A refreshing salad, displaying the colors of Hungary! Red, White and Green.

- 3 or 4 large juicy fresh tomatoes
- 1 cucumber peeled, scored with a fork and thick sliced
- 2 banana peppers sliced or 1 green pepper seeded and chopped
- 1/8 cup of chopped Italian flat leaf parsley -OR- 1 tsp. of minced fresh dill
- 1 small peeled onion sliced thin
- 1 garlic clove minced
- 3 Tbs. of vinegar
- 1 tsp. sugar
- 6 Tbs. of oil
- Salt and pepper

Slice the tomatoes and place in salad bowl. Peel cucumber, score lengthwise and slice. Slice the banana peppers or chopped seeded green pepper. Add the chopped parsley or dill, sliced onion, minced clove and toss together. Add to bowl vinegar, sugar and oil. Toss again, taste and adjust seasoning by adding salt and pepper if needed. Let sit for 1/2 hour to mingle flavors.

Authentic Hungarian Sour Cream Cole Slaw (Tejfeles kaposztasalata)

There are two kinds of cole slaw served in Hungarian households. One is the oil and vinegar slaw that is usually served in Winter, and the other is this recipe for sour cream cole slaw that does not contain any oil. It is a light, refreshing slaw, creamy and zesty. A perfect salad to accompany a summer meal.

- 1 cabbage head
- 1/2 small onion
- 2 Tbls. very finely chopped green pepper
- 2 or 3 Tbls. good white vinegar
- 16 oz. real sour cream
- sugar
- salt and pepper
- paprika

Slice cabbage head into slaw. Place slaw into bowl. Mince 1/2 small onion and add to bowl. Add 2 Tbls. chopped green pepper. Add 2 or 3 Tbl. white vinegar. Add 16 oz. real sour cream. Add 1 tsp. sugar. Add salt, about 1/2 tsp. Wash hands and take off rings. Place your hands into the slaw, mix and squeeze the slaw so it makes some juice. This will make the slaw limp. Taste, add more salt if needed. Add more vinegar if more "bite" is wanted. Sprinkle Paprika on top for beauty. Refrigerate till serving time. Good the next day also.

Serves 4 to 6.

Sour Cream Potato Salad (Tejfeles krumplisalata)

In summer we usually made and ate cold Sour Cream Potato Salad. In winter we made and ate Hot Bacon Potato Salad. This is a traditional Hungarian summer Potato Salad, made with sour cream instead of mayonnaise. It seems my teen aged life was spent in peeling potatoes either cooked or raw. We made tons of Potato Salad. It was inexpensive, it kept well, and everyone liked it. It also went well with everything from plain cooked hot dogs, to home baked hams.

- 8 good sized red potatoes
- 1 small onion minced
- 2 ribs of celery, sliced thin
- 4 eggs hard boiled and peeled
- 1/4 cup of pimento or fresh red pepper diced
- 2 cups sour cream, **or instead use:**
  (*non-traditional but excellent* - 1 cup sour cream and 1 cup mayonnaise)
- 1/4 cup of good white vinegar
- 1 heaping Tbs. of sugar (do not omit)
- 1/2 tsp. salt
- pepper

Wash potatoes and cook in boiling water until tender. Do not over cook or salad will get mushy. Drain potatoes, cool and peel. Slice into small pieces and place in mixing bowl with minced onion, sliced celery, chopped eggs, and diced pimento. Into bowl with these ingredients place the sour cream, vinegar, sugar and salt. Mix all with two large spoons, or as grandma did with your hands. Taste, if more salt is needed, add and add a few dashes of pepper. Let the Potato Salad rest in the refrigerator for a few hours to blend flavors. Put into a serving dish. Sprinkle a little Paprika on top and sprinkle some chopped flat parsley on for beauty. Serve cold.

Authentic Hungarian Beef Soup (Marha husleves)

This is a traditional winter soup. It is served in three courses. First the broth is served with fine or broad egg noodles, Tarhonya or Spaetzle. Then the meat and vegetables are served along with a cold sourcream and horse-radish sauce. This is a slow cooking soup, that tastes wonderful. It is worth the time it takes. It makes a cold winter day cosy. This serves a family.

- 2 lbs. beef chuck, in one piece
- 5 qts. cold water
- 3 tsp. salt
- 1/2 tsp. black pepper corns
- 6 whole carrots, cleaned
- 3 ribs of celery, cut in half
- 3 parsley root, peeled, cut in half and parsley greens
- 2 parsnips, peeled, cut in half
- 3 med. onions washed but unpeeled
- 6 whole cloves
- 3 potatos, peeled and halved

Sear meat in pot. (This gives greater flavor and color) Cover with water. Let it come to a boil and skim the foam off. Add salt, pepper corns, and let simmer for 1 hour. Stick 2 cloves into each onion. Add the carrots, celery, parsley root and greens, parsnips and onions. Cover and simmer slowly for about 2 hours. Add potatos last hour of cooking. Serve strained soup broth with your choice of noodles or Spaetzle. Arrange vegetables and meat on serving platter. Serve meat and vegetables with Sour Cream and Horse-Radish sauce, Tomato Sauce or Dill Sauce. Add some crusty bread and enjoy a wonderful meal.

Serves 4 to 6.

Authentic Hungarian Chicken Soup (Csirkeleves or Tyukleves)

Winter is the time for Chicken Soup. Wind and snow whipping around the yard. Windows get all steamed. Write your name on the mist. Smells that you will recognize in later years with a tug on your heart. There is no soup as good as the soup Mama made when you were young.

I remember going to the Poultry Store with my Grandma to buy live chickens. The man in the store would kill it for you by twisting its neck quickly, then dunking it in a vat full of boiling water, and someone would pull off the feathers. Grandma would take it home to cut out the guts and cut off the head and feet. Oh My! How that poultry store smelled. And noisy, with all the crates with live ducks and chickens and geese quacking. We children were always very curious to see if there were any unlaid eggs in the chicken. And how we teased one another with the cut off chicken feet. By pressing a spot on the foot you could make the claws open and close. We all watched as she singed off any remaining feathers by holding the chicken over the open gas flame. Those were the good old days? That was a lot of work! But the chickens then tasted much better than the chickens today.

- 1 fat hen or chicken parts disjointed (about 5 lbs.)
- 4 or 5 carrots, whole
- 1 whole parsley root with greens on top
- 1 or 2 onions each stuck with a whole clove
- 2 or 3 ribs of celery
- 1 small whole tomato
- 4 qts. of water
- 1 1/2 Tbls. salt
- 1/4 tsp. fresh ground black pepper
- 1/8 tsp. of mace

Cook chicken in pot with water, skiming the scum off when starting soup to boil. Place all the vegetables and spices in the pot. Cook under a low flame until the chicken is tender. Remove as much fat as possible. Strain soup and serve with broad noodles or LIVER DUMPLINGS. Eat chicken on the side with TOMATO SAUCE or DILL SAUCE.

LIVER DUMPLINGS

- 1 raw chicken liver chopped fine
- 4 sprigs of parsley greens, minced
- 1 small onion, minced
- 4 whole eggs
- 1/2 Tbls. salt
- 2 cups of flour

Mix all the ingredients together. A cusinart is great for this. Drop into boiling water by the 1/2 teaspoonsful. Cook about 15 minutes or until done. If batter is too thick you can add a little water. Drain and serve with soup.

Serves a family.

Authentic Hungarian Egg Noodles (Tojas teszta)

I still have in my possession my grandmother's wooden noodle and dough board. Brought from Hungary in the early 1900's, it was already worn by years of use. I remember her kneading bread or noodle dough on the board that was made to hook over the edge of a table so that the kneading movement of the dough would not crash the board to the floor.

My grandmother's kitchen had few accouterments for cooking. It contained a white porcelain sink on four legs, no hot water, an old cream and green colored porcelain gas stove on legs with a small chamber for baking. She had a small white enamel topped kitchen table with one small drawer for cutlery. Two chairs and an Ice box that was always dripping. There was a small coal burning stove in the corner of the kitchen, the sole heat source for the three room, cold water, shared bath, flat.

Out of this simple basic 1920's kitchen came the most wonderful smells and tastes. Noodles were not available in the little neighborhood stores. It would take another five years before Mr. Asian would start making wonderful egg noodles in his basement for sale to stores.

Chicken soup meant homemade noodles. Grandma would knead the stiff dough on her board until it was elastic. After she had rolled it out thinly with her heavy rolling pin, she would gently roll it up and using her sharpest knife, slice it into fine noodles. Then she would prop up a broom handle across the two chairs and hang the noodles like tinsel to dry.

- 3 eggs lightly beaten
- 3 cups of flour

In a bowl, mix the eggs and flour to make a stiff dough. Knead very well on floured surface until the dough is smooth and elastic. Cover dough with a plastic wrap and let it sit for 15 minutes. When dough has relaxed, use floured rolling pin to roll out very thin on the floured surface. Let the dough sit for a few minutes, then loosely roll up the thin dough and cut very fine with a sharp knife. If the noodles are very fine, you can fluff them up on your board and let them dry by occasionally tossing them.

If you are making broad noodles, you will want to let them hang to dry. If you do not have a noodle drying rack or a broom handle to prop somewhere, you can use a few hangers that have a cardboard tube on them.

When they are dry, cook in salted boiling water uncovered till tender, about 10 minutes or until soft. Drain in strainer or colander and add to soup.

Authentic Hungarian Farina Dumplings (Daragaluska)

Every ethnic cuisine has it's own way of economically stretching a meal. For eastern Europeans the dumpling is king. Every goulash, every soup, every paprikas, every sauerkraut and even desserts had its own particular type of dumpling. Soft, spongy, chewy, al dente, silky, what ever your desire. Farina dumplings are firmer to the bite than the flour kind. They are a wonderful addition to a chicken, beef or tomato soup. Very easy to make.

- 2 Tbl. butter
- 2 eggs
- Farina
- 1/4 teas. salt

Mix the soft butter, salt and the 2 eggs well. Add farina 1/4 cup at a time till you have a dumpling dough consistency. Then add a little soup for moisture. When the soup boils, cut the dumplings into the soup with a teaspoon. When they come to the top, cook about 5 minutes more.

Serves 4.

June Meyer's Authentic Hungarian Green Bean Soup (Zoldbableves)

The end of the growing season, when the green beans are putting out the last of their progeny, is a good time to use up the surplus and make Green Bean Soup. We would be getting tired of cooked green beans with butter, green beans with dill and creamed green beans. Green Bean Soup, a meal in a bowl, was a welcome change. For some reason, it was always made with green beans, not the wonderful yellow wax beans we also grew and loved. Originally, this green bean soup would be cooked for 4 or 5 hours, till the green beans looked a ghastly gray. Today, we know so much more about preserving food values, vitamins and fresh vegetables flavor. This soup cooks in about an hour.

Today, you can buy fresh green beans at any time of the year and make this wonderful hearty soup. You can make one of two variations:

Green Bean Soup with Hungarian Smoked Bacon using 3/4 lb. of smoked bacon

OR

Green Bean Soup with Hungarian Smoked Sausage using 1 lb. of smoked sausage cut in slices

- 1 lb. of Hungarian smoked sausage, cut into slices **OR** 3/4 lb. of Hungarian smoked bacon
- 2 or 3 lbs. of fresh green beans trimmed of ends and cut into 2 inch sections
- 3 small or 1 very large onion chopped
- 3 raw potatoes, peeled and chopped in chunks
- 3 quarts of water
- 1 Tbs. of salt
- 1/4 tsp. pepper corns
- 1 cup of sour cream
- 2 Tbs. of flour for thickening if needed
- 2 Tbs. good white vinegar

For Green Bean Soup with bacon, cut bacon off rind with knife and cut into 1/2 inch cubes. Sauté bacon cubes and rind in soup pot with chopped onion till onion is glossy. Add the trimmed green beans, chopped potatoes, water, salt and pepper corns. Bring to a boil, and simmer for about 1 hour; beans and potatoes should be tender. Lower heat, and in a small bowl, mix flour with 1 cup of sour cream, stir 1/2 cup of hot soup into the bowl with the flour/sour cream mixture and stir well, then add this to the hot soup to cream and thicken it. (Hot soup in the sour cream mix will prevent the sour cream from curdling if thrown into the hot soup with out this step). After soup has thickened, stir in the white vinegar and serve in large soup bowls, along with a good crusty white bread, or a dark pumpernickel bread.

For Green Bean Soup with smoked Hungarian sausage, sauté onions till glossy in a few tablespoons of lard, butter, or oil. Add the sliced Hungarian sausage and follow the recipe starting with the addition of green beans, potatoes, etc.

Makes 6 to 8 servings.

Authentic Hungarian style Sweet and Sour Cabbage Soup (Paradicsomos kaposztaleves)

Hungarian style Sweet and Sour Cabbage Soup takes advantage of the very flavorful broth or cooking liquid remaining after cooking butt made in the Austrian-Hungarian style. The butt is cooked in brown sugar water. (See Smoked Butt Hungarian Style) I usually make the butt and the Sweet and Sour Cabbage Soup on the same day, but serve the soup the next day. It is a hearty and filling soup, a favorite with the children.

Into reserved smoked pork butt and brown sugar cooking liquid, add:

- 2 onions peeled and chopped
- 1 small head of cabbage, cored and chopped
- 4 peeled and seeded ripe tomatoes **-OR-** 1 28 oz. can of crushed or whole tomatoes
- 2 cloves of garlic, optional
- 2 potatoes, peeled and chopped or grated (gives the soup a silky "feel")
- 5 whole pepper corns
- 2 whole cloves

Nice to add any left over smoked butt. Cover pot and bring to a boil, lower heat and slowly cool until cabbage and potatoes are soft (about 1 1/2 hours). Adjust seasoning, add salt if needed, add more brown sugar if needed. The soup should have a sweet (from the brown sugar) and sour (from the acid in the tomatoes). If you like, you can add a tablespoon of good white vinegar or the juice of half a lemon to make it more sour. Should be thick and full bodied.

Serve with a dollop of sour cream, crusty bread, and beer for a hearty meal.

Authentic Hungarian Lentil Soup (Lencseleves)

Hungarian soups are usually served in the fall and winter months. When ever I make a large pot of soup in winter, the steam always condenses on the windows. I then always think of a remote memory I have of playing by a low window, water running down in little riverlets, and shadowy forms passing by single file on the other side of the window, and the wonderful smell of soup cooking. When I asked my mother about the memory she said that my paternal grandmother had died in January 1936, and family and guests were coming back from the cemetery after the burial. It was frigid out and Hungarian soup, bread and Strudel was made to feed the frozen mourners. I was two years old and that faint memory has stayed with me for my whole life.

Never a separate course by itself, but always the main course. This is another one of those hearty Peasant soups that is a complete meal by itself. Serve it with some crusty bread, a chunk of cheese and a dark beer. Serve in a large bowl steaming hot.

- 1 lb. dried lentils, washed and drained
- 1/4 cup of lard, bacon drippings, or oil
- 2 medium onions, chopped
- 1 parsnip or parsley root, chopped
- 2 medium carrots, sliced
- 1 cup sliced celery
- 8 cups water
- 1 tsp. salt to taste
- several whole black pepper corns
- 2 whole cloves
- 2 bay leaves
- 1 large potato, peeled and grated

- 2 large links, or 4 small links smoked sausage, skin pricked with fork
- 2 Tbls. good vinegar

In a large pot, heat fat and add carrots, root vegetable and onions. Saute until onions are golden. Add lentils, water, celery, and seasonings. Grate the potato into the mixture and add sausage. Simmer covered 1 hour until lentils and vegetables are tender. Remove bay leaves. Add vinegar just before serving and adjust salt. Serve with a crusty bread and salad.

Mongol Soup

If you add one can of tomato paste and two cans of water to the above soup and puree it, you will have made another soup called Mongo Soup. Try it, it is good.

Serves 6.

Authentic Hungarian Liver Dumplings (Majgomboc)

Great Aunt Miller was my Grandfather Sehne's sister. A wonderful cook, she was a large woman and hard of hearing. It seems like she was always shouting as though we were the ones that were deaf. But when she shouted "liver dumplings ready" we were already seated patiently at the table. We waited for a large bowl of chicken soup, full of chicken bits, and wonderful liver dumplings. Nothing can compare with the taste of those fresh parsley and chicken liver dumplings, cut into the simmering soup. Easy to make, hard to forget.

- 4 chicken livers or 2 slices of calf's liver
- 1 Tbls. butter
- 1 egg
- 1 cup of flour
- 1/2 small onion
- 2 Tbls. of chopped parsley
- 1/2 tsp. salt and dash pepper

Cream butter and egg very throughly. Add flour till you have a nice dough. You may add a little more flour if needed. Grate the onion into the dough. Finely chop parsley into dough. Add 1/2 tea. salt and dash of pepper. Chop liver very fine. Add liver to dough. Cut into soup with teaspoon when the soup boiling.

Serves 4.

Modern Potato Dumplings

Yes, I know this is not traditional. But it is easy, fast and delicious.If you want a potato dumpling without a lot of fuss, use this recipe. Most people can not tell that they were made with instant potato flakes.

- 2 cups of instant potato flakes
- 2 eggs
- 2 cups of flour
- 2 cups of water

Mix in a bowl. Drop by spoonfuls into salted boiling water.
Cook until dumplings look done when cut in half, about 5 or 6 minutes.
Drain and serve with the Paprikas.

Serves 6 to 8.

Note: If you do not like dumplings, you can serve this with some cooked wide egg noodles.

Authentic Hungarian Potato Soup (Krumplileves)

This is another Hungarian fall and winter soup. Made with just celery, onions, potato and paprika sausage, and topped with vinegar and sour cream it is a hearty soup. It contains a surprise ingredient. When the soup is almost finished cooking, raw eggs are cracked into the hot soup to coddle. The Bay leaves are an important flavor ingredient. Do not omit them. This is an easy soup to make, and its flavor is unique. It has been a favorite in my family for many generations.

- 1 small whole stalk of celery, cut in small pieces, about 2 cups
- 2 onions, peeled and chopped
- 2 Tbls. chopped parsley leaves
- 3 Tbls. oil, (I use corn or peanut oil)
- 5 medium potatos, peeled and cut in small cubes
- 1 smoked Hungarian sausage cut into 2 inch chunks
  (**OR** mild pepperoni which is the closest to smoked Hungarian sausage)
- 1/4 tsp. black pepper corns
- 3 small **OR** 2 large bay leaves
- 2 quarts of water
- 3 Tbls. of good white vinegar
- 6 raw eggs
- 1/2 pint of sour cream
- 1 tsp. salt (celery and the vinegar are naturally salty)

In soup pot, saute celery and onions in oil until limp. Add to soup pot parsley, potatos, Hungarian sausage chunks, pepper corns, Bay leaves and 2 quarts of water. Simmer slowly for at least one hour, until potatos are soft. Add the 3 Tbls. of vinegar. Taste and if soup does not have enought salt, add to taste. While soup is simmering, break 6 raw eggs, one egg at a time, into the pot. Space them so they will cook to a firm

stage, without touching one another.
Do not stir soup!

Serve soup, eggs and chunks of sausage in each soup plate.
Put a heaping tablespoon of sour cream in each plate.
Serve with good bread. Yum!

Serves 6.

Authentic Hungarian Rivilchas or Tarhonya for Soup

How I loved to eat Hungarian Beef Soup or Tomato Soup with Rivilchas. A tiny chewy dumpling for Hungarian soups, they were made fresh and cooked in the soup in the big stock pot after the meat and whole vegetables were removed to a separate serving platter. They cook up chewy, better than any noodle. My Mother would quickly mix the stiff dough and grate it into irregular gratings of dough.

Tarhonya can also be made in large bulk as the Ancient Hungarians made. These were dried hard and stored in a large container for years without spoiling.

- 3 cups of sifted flour
- 3 whole eggs
- 1 tsp. salt
- 3 1/2 egg shells of water

Mix the flour, eggs, salt and water together. Knead to make a stiff dough. You may add a little more water if the dough is too stiff. Grate on the medium side of a grater. Rivilchas or Tarhonya should be the size of dried peas. Let the Tarhonya dry for 1/2 hour and then add to boiling water 1/2 cup at a time and cook till done. Drain and serve in hot Beef Soup, hot Chicken Soup or Tomato Soup.

Note: If you have a large pot of boiling soup, you can cook these Rivilchas or Tarhonya in the soup.

Bulk Dried Tarhonya about 25 servings

- 2 pounds of flour
- 7 whole eggs
- 1 1/2 Tbs. salt

- 1 cup of water

In a small mixing bowl mix eggs with the water and salt. Beat well. Put the flour in a large mixing bowl and add the egg mixture a little at a time. Blend the dough with your hands in a rubbing motion as though you were washing your hands with the palms open. The mix should become uneven little pieces of dough the size of dried peas. Break up any that look large. The mix should be somewhat uniform. Spread out a tablecloth on a table and spread the Tarhonya on it in a thin layer so that all the pieces are exposed to the air. Let dry until very hard, this will take 3 or 4 days. While the mix is drying, roll your fingers through to mix it up so all sides are exposed to air. When you are sure that the mix has dried hard, store in a container.

Note: Make Tarhonya in the hot summer, never during a rainy season or the mix will never dry hard. If you have some particles that are larger and are not hard, sift them out and let them dry separately.

To Bake Dried Tarhonya - serves 6

Brown 1/2 cup of dried Tarhonya in 3 Tbs. of butter or lard. Add 1 tsp. of salt, 1 Tbs. Hungarian Paprika and water to cover. Cover and bake in the oven at 375 degrees. It will take about 35 minutes to 1 1/2 hours depending on the size and age of the dried Tarhonya. The water should be absorbed when the Tarhonya is cooked.

Serve instead of potato, noodles, dumplings or rice.

Authentic Hungarian Sour Cherry Soup (Meggyleves)

Every Family has their version of Sour Cherry Soup. It is a special seasonal treat in Hungary when the cherries are ripe. Sour Cherries have a wonderful flavor when cooked. Some families like to make their soup with sweet cream instead of sour cream. Some add a little sherry. How ever you make this soup, you will enjoy its refreshing flavor. I love a cold cup on summer evenings before going to bed. I have wonderful dreams. Peaches can be substituted for Cherries.

- 1 1/2 quarts of water
- 3 Tbs. flour
- 1 cup sour cream
- 1/2 tsp. of salt
- 1 pound of fresh or frozen pitted sour cherries or more (Do not use canned)
- 3/4 cup granulated sugar

Into a soup pot containing 1 1/2 quarts of boiling water add fresh or frozen sour cherries and granulated sugar. Stir and cook. In a separate bowl mix flour, sour cream, salt and beat until smooth. Add to flour mix, 1 cup of hot cherry sugar mix. Stir vigorously. Now add the flour, sour cream and hot cherry mix into the pot of hot soup, stir well and simmer for 5 or 6 minutes until it thickens. Cover the soup and let cool. Keep cover on while it chills in refrigerator and it will not form a thick skin. Serve very cold.

To make Cherry Soup with Sweet Cream or Meggyleves Mas Modon, cook a 1 inch stick of cinnamon with the cherries, and substitute sweet cream for the sour cream. Discard cinnamon stick when done cooking soup. Chill as above.

Note: Rinse the fresh cherries in water. Drain. Use your fingers to pluck out the pits. DO NOT lose a pit in the soup. Someone will break a tooth! Also, cover your upper body with an apron or towel, when pitting, or the fresh juice will splatter and stain your clothes.

Authentic Hungarian Spaetzle or Little Dumplings

There are many recipes for dumplings. Every family makes theirs a little different. Spaetzle are little dumpling, these are made with Farina or Cream of Wheat. They are firmer than an all flour Spaetzle. These are good in Chicken Soup, Tomato Soup, Chicken Paprikas, Beef Gulyas.

- 2 1/2 cups of all purpose flour
- 1 tsp. salt
- 2 Tbs. Cream of Wheat or Farina
- 2 eggs
- 3/4 cups of water
- 1 Tbs. butter melted

Put flour, salt, and cream of wheat into a bowl. Make a well in the middle and add the eggs, water and butter. Stir until batter is smooth and thick. Cut the batter by teaspoon full into a big pot of boiling salted water. Dip the spoon into the hot water each time to keep the batter from sticking to the spoon. Cook only half the batter at a time to avoid crowding. Stir the bottom of the pot with a wooden spoon so that the dumplings will rise to the top. After the dumplings rise, let them cook for 2 minutes.
Remove from the water and drain.

Serve warm.

Authentic Hungarian Split Pea Soup (Sargaborsoleves)

Hungarian pea soup is so thick and hearty you can spoon it up like a porridge. Sweet and flavorful, I have tasted many other pea soups, but this family recipe is most satisfying and memorable. This soup or porridge is full of sweet carrots, parsnips and parsley leaves and roots, onions, yellow peas and ham.

Winter and spring were always the times to make hearty pea soups. All the dried peas stored from the previous harvest were dwindling in number and the stored carrots, parsnips and parsley root were becoming sweet as they lost moisture in the root bin. As a child I can remember dreading having to go down into the root cellar which was cold and dark, and full of spider webs, to collect the roots for peas soup. My father had dug out the root cellar under our house in a neighborhood of Chicago bungalows that was built right after the Chicago Fire. It was inconceivable to any European immigrant not to have a dark, cold place to store food. In Europe there was no refrigeration. The root cellar under the house or the bubbling spring house if you were lucky to have one were the only cool places to store food in summer. The root cellar never froze in winter. Besides, roots and potatoes, we stored bushels of apples, squash, onions, crocks of sauerkraut, and home canned food and dried smoked Hungarian sausage.

- 1 lb. of split yellow peas
- 1 small ham shank or smoked pork butt
- 1 large onion chopped
- 4 med. carrots sliced
- 3 ribs of celery
- 1 parsley root diced
- 1/4 cup chopped flat leaf parsley
- 1 parsnip root diced
- 1 bay leaf
- 2 whole cloves

- 6 whole peppercorns
- 3 quarts of water
- 1/4 cup of pearl barley -optional-

Wash and drain yellow peas and place in soup pot with 3 quarts of cold water. Add ham or pork butt, along with vegetables and spices and optional barley. Bring water to a boil, turn down heat and slowly cook until all veggies and peas are soft. Taste for seasoning, and now add required salt. (Ham and pork butt are salty, do not add salt at the beginning of cooking). Cooking will take about an hour and a half. If the soup is not as thick as you like it, cook it a little longer. The soup should be thick, like a peas porridge. Serve in a large bowl with a slice of ham or pork butt in each serving. Add a crusty bread and salad for a satisfying one dish meal.

Makes 6 servings.

Authentic Hungarian Tomato Soup (Paradicsomleves)

Ah Paradise to eat Hungarian Tomato Soup. The tomato once feared as being poisonous, was also called the Paradice Appfel or Apple of Paradise. When my Grandmother came to this country from Austria-Hungary, she brought not only flower seeds, Poppies included, but all kinds of old-world tomato seeds. Hungarian heart shaped tomatos, heavy, sweet and succulent. It was a yearly ritual in late summer to can and bottle all those wonderful ripe tomatos the garden produced. All winter long we children would be sent down to the preserves cellar to bring up jars of tomatos, peppers, pickles, dilled squash, plums, peaches, beets, jams and jellies. Alas, I no longer have a garden so I must rely on store bought cans of tomatos.

Hungarian Pancakes, (Palacsinta) were always served after the soup course. Thin crepes, slathered with strawberry jam, rolled up and sprinkled with powdered sugar. This was a complete meal, good for a Saturday noon, or Sunday night. Ah Paradise!

- 1/2 lb. good bacon, sliced and cut in small pieces
- 1 large onion, minced
- 1 32 oz. can of crushed or pureed tomatos
- 1 can of water
- 1/2 cup of celery, minced
- 1 Tbls. sugar
- 8 peppercorns
- salt to taste

Saute bacon in a soup pot, and drain off bacon fat. Saute minced onion and celery with bacon bits in pot till transparent. Add the can of tomatos and add one can of water. Add 1 Tbls. sugar, and peppercorns. Bring soup pot to low boil, and lower heat to simmer and let simmer about 45 min. or 1hour. Soup can contain broad noodles, or rice. precook these and add before serving. Serves 4 to 6.

Authentic Hungarian Trickle Egg Noodles (Spaetzle)

There are as many variations of dumplings, noodles or spaetzle as there are variations of recipes for Goulash. Every family has at least three or four varieties that become the favorites of the family members.

Some go best with clear soups, others with creamy soups. If you want to keep your chicken or beef soup clear and not cloudy, cook the noodles or dumplings separately in water and then add to the soup.

These noodles or spaetzle go well with rich sauced dishes. See "Farina Dumplings" If you like a heartier and chewier dumpling.

- 2 cups flour or more if needed.
- 1/2 cup water
- 3 whole eggs
- 1 1/2 tsps. salt

Break eggs into bowl containing flour.
add water and 1 1/2 tsp. salt and mix dough thoroughly. Dough should not be very firm.

If you have a large holed colander you can push the dough through the holes with a rubber spatula to trickle into a large pot of boiling water. Do not cook all the noodles or spaetzle at one time, better to do two batches. Cook for 5 minutes and then drain, toss with some melted butter.

Serve with Chicken Paprikash, Beef Goulash, or anything that has a rich sauce.

Note: If you have a spaetzle maker, use over the boiling water.

Authentic Hungarian Beef Pot Roast with Vegetables (Zoldseges dinsztelt marhahus)

You could always tell when Beef Pot Roast with Vegetables was cooking in the oven. It has it's very own delectable smell which combines the browning meat with the roasting and browning vegetables. Your nostrils will flare open at the recognition of the smell and your mouth will water in anticipation of consuming this oldest of one pot cookery.

- 1 beef roast at least 3 lbs.
- 3 or 4 small whole peeled onions each stuck with a clove
- 2 ribs of celery cut into half
- 4 or 5 whole peeled carrots, cut in half
- 6 or 7 small whole peeled raw potatoes

Gravy

- 1 1/2 cups water
- 1 heaping tablespoon flour
- 1 Tbls. butter

Put a heavy pot on the burner with the heat on high. As soon as the pot is hot and the lard melted, put the meat in and sear (let it brown quickly) it on all sides. If the pot is really hot the meat will not stick, if it does, don't worry. Do Not salt, salting will draw too much liquid out of the meat and make it dry. You can pepper it, preferably with fresh ground pepper. Take pot off the stove, add the vegetable, put on the lid and put it in the oven (325) for about 2 hours. You can check on it and turn it over 1/2 way. DO NOT ADD WATER OR ANY THING ELSE. By the time your two hours are up, you should have a richly browned and tender piece of meat with roasted vegetables. (If it is not tender leave it in the covered pot in the oven with the heat turned off for another 1/2 hour). Remove the meat to a slicing board and the vegetable to a serving dish. Let the meat rest for about 15 minutes. While the meat is resting put the pot on the burner at medium heat, mix 1 1/2 cups of water with 1 heaping tablespoon of flour and stir it into the juices in the pot. Do not forget to scrape down the black sides of the pot with the gravy (this is the source of all that good caramel color and flavor.) Cook gravy a few minutes until thickened and add Tbls. of butter. Salt meat if needed, slice the meat and put back into the pot so that meat is covered with gravy before being served. Serve the vegetables on the side. This may seem long, but it is really simple and the best pot roast beef flavor possible. Just be aware that when you sear the meat your smoke alarm may go off.

A 3 lbs. roast with vegetables serves 4, a larger roast more.

Authentic Hungarian Cabbage and Noodles (Haluska)

Fresh Green Cabbage, that most versatile vegetable. Easy to keep for a long time in the bottom of the vegetable drawer or root cellar. Cheap and available all year long.

The farmers would bring in wagons loaded high with heads of green cabbage. They knew that their lives would depend on their putting enough cabbage away for the winter. Large crocks would be filled with shredded cabbage and salt to make sour kraut, and heads would be buried in straw bins in the root cellar.

Hungarians prepare cabbage in more different ways than any other ethnic cuisine. Cabbage can be eaten raw or cooked. Raw, in the various refreshing cold slaws, eaten in summer or winter. It is preserved and pickled with salt as sour kraut and made into many distinctive regional dishes. It is most delicate when sliced and sautéed with butter. The worst thing you can do to it, is boil it.

This dish exemplifies the delicacy of sautéed cabbage. It comes out nutty and buttery.

- 1 stick of butter
- 1 large onion peeled and cut in strips
- 1 small head of cabbage **OR** 1/2 large head of cabbage, cut into strips
- 1 tsp. salt
- 1/4 tsp. pepper
- 1 box or bag of large egg noodles, cooked and drained
- 1 pint of sour cream

Melt the butter in a large pan or pot, large enough to hold the chopped cabbage.
Sauté the cabbage and the onion in the butter until glossy and tender.
Now add the salt, pepper. Cover and let the cabbage mixture cook over low heat for about 15 minutes.

Add cooked drained egg noodles and mix.

Serve with bowl of sour cream. Add salt to taste.

Note: There is a variation that I make often. 1 lb. of cooked ground beef, **OR** 1 lb. of thinly sliced smoked Hungarian sausage, **OR** 1/2 lb. of cubed smoked Hungarian paprika bacon, sauted with onion and cabbage. This can be placed on top of the noodles and the cabbage.

Serves 4 to 6.

Authentic Hungarian Calfs Liver with Onions and Vinegar Sauce (Hagymas borjumjaj ecetesmartassal)

Mention calfs liver and a lot of people make strange faces. Serve Hungarian style calfs liver that was dipped in pakrika, and sauted in butter along with thinly sliced onions and then smothered in vinegar to make a most unusual but succulent dish. Serve with mashed potatos or cooked rice and you have heaven on earth.

- calfs liver
- sliced white or yellow onion (One for every two people eating)
- imported sweet paprika
- salt and pepper
- flour
- butter
- good vinegar (red or white)

Depending on how much liver you are making, slice liver into finger sized strips. Season liver with very liberal sprinkling of paprika. Season with salt and pepper. Dredge strips in flour. Let rest while you thinly slice onions. Melt butter in frying pan and saute onions. When onions are almost cooked, toss in the liver strips and saute along with the onions. The liver will only take a few minutes to cook. When they are done, sprinkle about 1/2 tsp. paprika over the onions and mix in a good Tbls. vinegar to make a thick onion gravy.

Serve when ready.

Chicken Paprika Stew with Tomato (Paprikas csirkeporkolt paradicsommal)

Chicken appears in Hungarian cookery often but it is never boring because there are so many ways to serve it. Authentic Chicken Paprikas never has tomatoes in it. Chicken Paprika Stew does. Make plenty of dumplings to go with it. It is so good.

- 2 onions chopped
- 4 Tbsp. shortening, corn oil or lard
- 3 Tbsp. Hungarian paprika
- 2 tsp. sugar, do not omit
- 1/8 Tsp. black pepper or whole pepper corns
- 1 bay leaf
- 2 Tsp. salt
- 4 to 5 lbs. chicken disjointed, use legs, thighs, breast and back for best flavor
- 1 large can of crushed tomatoes
- 2 cups water
- 2 Tbs. flour
- 2 Tbs. butter
- 1/2 pt. sour cream

Brown onions in shortening. Add seasonings and chicken, brown 10 minutes. Do not let burn. Add tomatoes, bay leaf and water, cover and let simmer slowly until it is tender. It will smell wonderful! To thicken gravy, mix into a paste 2 Tbs. soft butter with 2 Tbs. flour and stir into the stew liquid. Cook a few minutes until the liquid thickens. Serve with dumplings or wide noodles.

Top each serving with sour cream.

Authentic Hungarian Chicken Paprikas (Csirkepaprikas)

This dish is perhaps the Jewel in the Crown of Hungarian cuisine. My mouth salivates when I think of Paprikas. There is no finer dish to demonstrate what paprika tastes likes when it is slow cooked in a dish. It will bring tears of graditude to the eyes of the most jaded gourmet. Mind you, this dish was eaten by every family in Hungary when they could spare a chicken from egg production.

Every country household had a yard full of chickens. Chicken dishes that could be slow cooked on the stove for supper were plentiful. Paprikas was a dish for Sunday dinner or weekday supper. A pot of potato dumplings, and perhaps a platter of pickled hungarian peppers and a loaf of crusty home baked bread was all that was need for ones well being. Every meal was eaten with gusto.

- 2 onions chopped
- 4 Tbsp. shortening, corn oil or lard
- 3 Tbsp. Hungarian paprika
- 1/8 Tsp. black pepper or whole pepper corns
- 2 Tsp. salt
- 4 to 5 lbs. chicken disjointed, use legs, thighs, breast and back for best flavor
- 1 1/2 cups water
- 1/2 pt. sour cream

Brown onions in shortening. Add seasonings and chicken, brown 10 minutes. Add water, cover and let simmer slowly until it is tender. It will smell wonderful! Remove chicken, add sour cream to drippings in pan and mix well. To thicken gravy, mix into a paste 1 Tbl. soft butter with 1 Tbl. of flour and stir into drippings. Add dumplings and arrange chicken on top. Heat through, but do not boil, and serve.
(See Modern Potato Dumplings on page 57).

Authentic Hungarian Chicken and Rice (Rizses csirke aprolek)

Chicken and Rice was always a nice change from Goulash and Dumplings. It is a family dish, that was served from the stove. Simple but very good. Not a soup, not a casserole but something in between. Best made with gizzard, liver, wings, feet (where can you get feet today)? The bony parts and the skin impart a wonderful flavor and mouth feel that you cannot get without.

- 1 chicken cut up or equivalent, use all parts
- 1 large onion, diced
- 1 cup of celery thin sliced
- 1 cup of sliced carrots
- 1/4 cup of flat leafed parsley chopped
- 2 bay leaves
- 1 heaping cup of washed rice
- 2 or 3 Tbls. of lard
- 2 cups of water
- 1 1/2 tsp. salt
- 1/4 tsp. black peppercorns
- Sour cream

Use a heavy pot with lid, and sauté onions, celery and carrots in the lard until glossy. Add the cut up chicken to the vegetables and brown. Add the salt, water, bay leaves, parsley, pepper corns and simmer for at least 45 minutes over medium heat until the meat is almost tender.

Add the washed rice to the vegetable and chicken, stir, cover and cook slowly until the rice is tender. (about 20 min.) You may need to add additional water to prevent the rice from burning. Adjust salt.

Serve with a little sour cream and vinegar if desired. Serves 4 to 6.

Authentic Hungarian Farina and Noodles (Galuska es dara)

Hungarian peasants are masters of culinary arts. They can make sumptuous meals out of practically nothing. I remember meals we ate during the Great Depression that were meatless, (see Potatoes, Dumplings and Bread crumbs). I wrongly assumed that we ate these because they were inexpensive. Little did I know that these dishes were beloved by not only the Hungarian peasants but by the affluent as well. Farina and Noodles can be a lunch dish, or a dessert dish. It is unique in that the farina is toasted to give it a very unusual taste. It has a toasted nut flavor that combined with butter and brown sugar produce a very likable dish. One of those "the more I eat, the more I want" dish. It is traditionally served with a cooked or canned fruit.

- 1 package of broad egg noodles about 8 ounces
- 1/2 cup of uncooked farina
- 1/2 stick of butter or 4 Tbls. butter
- 1/2 cup of cold water
- 2 or three heaping Tbs. brown sugar
- salt to taste

Start the broad egg noodles to cook in 2 quarts of boiling salted water
In a dry frying pan over moderate heat, toast the farina to a nice light brown color by swirling and shifting the pan. Do not use high heat or you will char the farina.
After the farina is toasted, add the butter, and mix well with the farina.
Add the water to the farina mix in the pan, and stir over medium heat until the farina starts to get creamy.
Add 2 heaping Tbls. of brown sugar, mix in well, cook for a few minutes until the farina is tender.
Add the cooked drained noodles to the pan, toss and mix well.
Cover pan and let the mixture cook for about 10 minutes over a low flame. The farina should form a crispy crust on the bottom. Serve with a dish of cooked fruit, like peaches or pears, plums or cherries. Serves 2.

Authentic Hungarian Fried Chicken (Sultcsirke)

I can remember when chicken was purchased at the Poultry Store instead of the modern supermarket. It was killed, gutted and de feathered at the store. Grandma had to work on it at the gas stove singeing off any feathers that the store missed. The neck, back, feet, head, wings and innards were cooked in water for a small soup. (older hens were purchased for a big soup).

For some unknown reason, Fried chicken was a Sunday dish. We never had fried chicken on any other day. It was always a favorite meal. For Sunday dinners we always had a tablecloth, ate in the Dinning room and had a special dessert. Always homemade. Apple Strudel with whipped cream, Hot milk Chocolate Cake, Hungarian pastries all eaten on the "Good dishes" that we got free at the neighborhood movie theaters. It was not until my parents 25th Wedding Anniversary that they finally received "Really Good Dishes" as gifts along with some silver plate cutlery.

- 2 or 3 lbs. of cutup chicken trimmed of any extra hanging fat or loose skin
- 2 whole beaten eggs
- 1 cup of flour
- 2 cups of fine white bread crumbs
- salt
- pepper
- 3 or 4 Tbls. lard

Generously salt and pepper the chicken pieces.
Dip the pieces of chicken into a dish of the flour, coat all sides and shake off the excess flour. The flour coating will help the egg coating to adhere.
Dip the pieces of floured chicken into the dish of the beaten raw egg and coat all sides. Press the pieces chicken into a bowl of fine white bread crumbs. Coat all sides with crumbs.

If you run out of flour, egg or bread crumbs, just add more to plates.

Heat the lard in a large frying pan. Lard has the advantage of not scorching as easily as butter and lard makes a tastier browned coating.

Sauté the pieces over a moderate heat until they are a golden brown. You do not want to crowd the chicken or you will steam it instead of brown it. You will know when to turn it over, the bottom breading will be a golden brown. Carefully turn over the chicken pieces and let the other side brown. The chicken will smell done, and the juices will be clear not pink if you prick it with a fork.
Do not cover finished chicken completely with a cover. The steam will soften the bread crumb coating and it will fall off. You can make an A frame tent of foil to hold the heat without steaming and making the chicken soggy.

Note: The white meat or breast pieces of chicken will cook in half the time that the dark or legs and thighs will cook. If you have a lot of chicken and small frying pans, cook the dark meat and the white meat in separate pans.

Authentic Hungarian Goulash (Gulyasleves)

Here is a recipe for authentic Hungarian Goulash I learned to make from my grandmother and mother who were from Austria-Hungary. Every family has its own version of Goulash. My family would NEVER consider tomatos or green peppers or other spices in Goulash. Some other dishes would have tomato or green pepper, but not Goulash. Slow cooking is the secret and you can never use too much paprika. I like to use 3 tablespoons. Hope you enjoy this dish, I have been raised on it.

- 2 lb. beef chuck
- 1 tsp. salt
- 2 onions, white or yellow
- 2 Tbsp. lard or shortening
- 2 Tbsp. imported sweet paprika
  (most important to use real hungarian paprika for ultimate favor)
- 2 bay leaves
- 1 qt. water
- 4 peeled and diced potatoes
- 1/4 tsp. black pepper

Cut beef into 1 inch squares, add 1/2 tsp. salt. Chop onions and brown in shortening, add beef and paprika. Let beef simmer in its own juice along with salt and paprika for 1 hr. on low heat. Add water, diced potatoes and remaining salt. Cover and simmer until potatoes are done and meat is tender. Prepare egg dumpling batter:

Egg dumpling batter

- 3 eggs

- 1 1/2 cups flour
- 3/4 tsp. salt

Add flour to unbeaten egg and salt. Mix well. Let stand for 1/2 hour for flour to mellow. Drop by teaspoonful into Goulash. Cover and simmer 5 minutes after dumplings rise to surface.

Serve hot with dollops of sour cream.

Authentic Hungarian Gypsy Bacon (Ciganyszalonna or Zigeunerspeck)

My father was born in Transylvania. His Grandfather taught him how to make Gypsy Bacon over the campfire the same way that shepherds had made it for a thousand years.

I remember sitting around the camp fire in the local Forest Preserve, holding a stick with a chunk of smoked bacon over the coals. Potatos were buried in the embers and opened cans of pork and beans were standing on stones in the campfire. Someone was alway dropping their bacon on the dirt or the grass. Pick it up and burn off the dirt. Eat it. Delicious.

Prepare a smoked cured slab of bacon, with the rind still attached, by scoring it in 1 inch square sections down to the rind. Cut off a 3 by 3 inch secton for each person. Skewer it on a long fork or stick and hold it over the fire until the bacon starts to cook and sizzle. Let the aromatic bacon fat drip onto a thick slice of rye bread. The rind will shrink and curls up the bacon sections. Is your mouth watering yet? Sprinkle paprika over bacon, eat by cutting off an inch cube with a knife and topping it with chopped sweet onion on the hearty rye bread. Serve with cold beer and Schnapps chasers. The taste is wonderful, good on those cold nights around the campfire.

This type of bacon can be bought at german or hungarian deli or meat markets. The bacon is firm, not soft. It is cured in a way which permits you to also eat it raw in thin slices on bread as an appetizer.

Authentic Hungarian Hamburgers (Labdapecsenye)

In old world families, "Hamburgers for dinner" meant a hearty mound of meat, fried in fat until it had a rich brown flavorful crust. It was served as a meal for dinner, along with a vegetable dish, and mashed potato. In Austria-Hungary the Hamburger was carried to new heights. This was not a simple "make a thin flat patty and fry" recipe. A secret to the best flavor is to fry them in Lard!

- 1/2 lb. ground beef (if you do not want pork, use 1 lb. ground beef)
- 1/2 lb. ground pork
- 4 slices of white bread
- 1 tsp. salt
- 2 raw eggs
- 1 small onion finely chopped
- 1 clove of garlic, mashed
- 2 Tbls. of fresh parsley, minced (use Italian flat parsley for best flavor)
- 1/2 tsp. ground black pepper
- 1/2 cup water
- lard or oil

Saute chopped onion in a little fat or oil. Wet bread with water, tear into small pieces. In mixing bowl beat eggs well. Add meat, bread and the rest of the ingredients and mix lightly with your hands. Form mixture into medium sized balls, about 5 or 6. Flatten slightly. Fry SLOWLY in 1/2 inch of Crisco, lard or oil until tender and all sides are nicely browned and some what crispy. Let each side cook before attemping to turn with spatula. Serve hamburgers hot along with a potato and vegetable dish, and perhaps Hungarian cucumber salad. (you can double the recipe for robust eaters. Leftovers are good the next day cold!) Honest!
Serves 4

Authentic Hungarian Sausage
(Kolbasz)

My father was only 5 years old when he came to America from Romainia in 1905. He made sausage, wine, beer, smoked bacon, and all the Hungarian dishes that were brought to America by my maternal relations. He had a gusto for life. Everything he did he did when whistling. You knew he was happy.

Our city house always had a small smoke house at the back of the yard. It was used to sugar cure bacon the hungarian way, and to smoke links of Hungarian Sausage. My father would make sausage when it got cold out, and we would eat some fresh cooked, and the rest would be smoked and dried like pepperoni to be used in Potato Soup or Sauerkraut dishes all winter long. (The fresh sausage freezes well. Years ago we did not have large freezer, so sausage was smoked to keep good).

This sausage is heavy on garlic and paprika. If you do not have a sausage stuffer you can still make this sausage by making patties and frying it in a pan. The recipe that follows is for fresh sausage.

- 10 lbs. coarse ground pork butt or pork shoulder
- 1/3 cup imported mild Hungarian paprika. (Do not substitute generic)
- 1/4 cup salt
- 2 Tbls. ground black pepper
- 1 or 2 heaping Tbls. ground allspice (use 2 if you want it spicy)
- 5 or 6 garlic cloves
- 2 cups water

Bring water to boil, add peeled cloves of garlic and simmer 20 minutes. Fish out cloves of garlic and mash them with a little water. Add this to remaining water and mix all of the garlic water into the meat mix. Mix everything together well. Keep the meat mix cool. If you stuff the mix into casings, let the sausages hang for a day in at least 20 degrees. Smoke sausage according to your smoker instructions. If you are not going to stuff into casings, form into patties, wrap and freeze.

HOW TO COOK HUNGARIAN SAUSAGES

Take as many fresh links as needed and place in a heavy frying pan with a cover. Pour water over the sausages so the links are in 1/2 inch of water. Cover. Start the water to a slow boil, turn down the heat and simmer the sausage in the water until the sausage starts to take on color. Turn the sausage over and add a little more water to keep it from burning. When both sides are brownish, leave the cover off and continue cooking slowly to cook away any remaining water. The sausage should be a nice rich red brown. The aroma will be heavenly. We always serve with cold SOUR CREAM AND HORSERADISH SAUCE. Potatos and a sauerkraut dish go well with this dish too.

Dried and smoked sausage is used like pepperonni.

My brother Frank Wischler of Lombard, Illinois, carries on the tradition of sausage making. He makes ITALIAN SAUSAGE by leaving out the PAPRIKA and the ALLSPICE. Instead he uses 2 ounces of whole FENNEL SEED that has been cooked in a little water to soften the seeds and make the flavor more pronounced.

Authentic Hungarian Style Pot Roast (Fott marhahus)

What can one say about Pot Roast. It is usually an inexpensive piece of tough meat, that is without real character. Hungarian Style Pot Roast is still an inexpensive piece of meat, but it is the Cinderella of the kitchen. Pot Roasts are often dry and stringy. This pot roast is juicy, flavorful, tender and resting in a wonderful, natural gravy, rich in color and flavor.

- one pot roast any size, trimmed of most of the fat
- 1 1/2 cups of water
- 1 heaping Tbl. flour
- salt and pepper

Put a heavy pot on the burner with the heat on high. As soon as the pot is hot, put the meat in and sear (let it brown quickly) it on all sides. If the pot is really hot the meat will not stick, if it does, don't worry. Do Not salt, but you can pepper it, preferably with fresh ground pepper. Take pot off the stove, put on the lid and put it in the oven (325) for about 2 hours. You can check on it and turn it over 1/2 way. DO NOT ADD WATER OR ANY THING ELSE. By the time your two hours are up, you should have a richly browned and tender piece of meat. (If it is not tender leave it in the covered pot in the oven with the heat turned off for another 1/2 hour). Remove the meat to a slicing board and let it rest for about 15 minutes. While the meat is resting put the pot on the burner at medium heat, mix 1 1/2 cups of water with 1 heaping tablespoon of flour and stir it into the juices in the pot. Do not forget to scrape down the black sides of the pot with the gravy (this is the source of all that good caramel color and flavor). Salt if needed, slice the meat and put back into the pot so that meat is covered with gravy before being served. This may seem long, but it is really simple and the best pot roast beef flavor possible. Just be aware that when you sear the meat your smoke alarm may go off.

Authentic Hungarian Jellied Pigs Feet (Kocsonyas sertescsulok)

As a young child, I remember my Father bringing home pigs feet to cook. I never felt an aversion to them as do so many other people who were not raised on them. We used to eat cold homemade Jellied Pigs feet often. Succulent little split feet surrounded by flavorful melt in your mouth aspic. We would sprinkle little drops of vinegar over them. They were very good.

Once in a while my father would bring home a whole pigs head and he would make Head Cheese. That pigs head I felt an aversion to. There is just something about a pigs head sitting on the kitchen table. I love Head Cheese and will often buy a one inch thick slice and sprinkle it with vinegar and eat it with a slice of rye bread for lunch. I do not make Head Cheese.

- 2 1/2 or 3 lbs. of small or medium sized pigs feet, scrubbed clean and split
- 2 medium sized oinions, peeled
- 2 large carrots, sliced
- 3 cloves of peeled whole garlic
- 2 tsp. of good Hungarian paprika
- 2 tsp. of salt
- 1 Tbs. of pickling mixed spice

Put pigs feet into 2 quarts of water and bring to a boil. Throw away water. Wash off feet in cold water. Add another 2 quarts of cold water and the onions, carrots, garlic, paprika, salt and mixed spice.

Note: If you like a very firm jelly or aspic, add some veal bones when you cook the feet.

Cook for about 3 hours or until feet become tender. Keep skimming the water to keep the broth clear. Put feet into a serving dish that will fit into the refrigerator. Strain the broth and then pour over the feet, and chill.

Sprinkle with some paprika. Serve with a good hearty bread, pickled peppers, good German beer, and a small decanter of good vinegar to sprinkle on feet if desired.

Serves 5 to 7

Authentic Hungarian Kaiser Schmarren (Czaszar morzsa)

Kaiser's Schmarren tanslates loosely to "Emperor's Pain". It was a dish we would have for supper on those days when we wanted a break from meat or poultry dishes. It's name comes from the stories of how Franz Joseph, the Emperor of Austria-Hungary, would emit groans of pleasure when he ate this pancake like dish. Oooooooo, Ummmmmmmm, Ahhhhhhh! At any rate, it is a very good dish for a summer or winters eve. It is always served with a side dish of fresh fruit or cooked fruit like plums, cherries or peaches, or a side dish of Hungarian Cucumber Salad.

- have ready a cast iron pot or a heavy pot
- 3 cups flour
- 4 whole eggs
- 1 tsp. salt
- 1/2 cup sugar
- not quite 1/2 quart of milk
- 1/4 cup melted butter
- 3 heaping Tbls. lard
- confection sugar

In a bowl mix the flour, 4 eggs, salt, milk and melted butter. Mix with a whisk until smooth. Melt the lard in the pot, get it very hot! Pour in all the batter at once and cook it as a large pancake, over high heat. As it cooks lift up the edges of the pancake to let the uncooked batter flow underneath. When it is completely set, pull apart the pancake with the spatula and turn pieces over to cook on the other side. The pancake pieces should have some browned edges. This dish only takes a few minutes to make, but you must stay with it if you do not want to have charred pieces. Pile onto a serving dish, and sprinkle the top with powdered sugar. Serve with cooked fruit on the side, or cucumber salad. Sometimes for a change, you can add 3/4 cup of softened raisins to the batter for a sweet Schmarren. Serves 4.

Authentic Hungarian Kidney Stew (Veseporkolt)

Hungarians raised a lot of pigs to eat. Their bacon and hams are world famous. Every part of the pig was used. Nothing was ever thrown away. Pork kidneys make a wonderful stew and we would eat this stew often over cooked potatoes or dumplings.

The last time my Mother made Kidney Stew her pressure cooker blew up. We had Kidney stew dripping from the ceiling, and puddles of Kidney stew on the floor. What a mess! It was even in our hair. It was a long time before she made Kidney Stew again. Certainly not in her pressure cooker.

- 5 or 6 pork kidneys
- 1 large onions, chopped
- 4 Tbs. lard
- 1 Tbs. paprika
- 1/2 tsp. salt
- a little black pepper
- 2 bay leaves
- good pinch of mace
- enough water to cover
- 2 Tbs. flour
- 2 Tbs. soft butter
- sour cream
- dumplings or cooked potatoes

Soak Kidneys in milk for an hour and discard milk. Dry kidneys and remove any membrane or tubes or tough tissue and as much fat as possible. Slice kidneys and cut in small cubes (smaller than dice). Into stew pot, melt 4 Tbs. of lard and cook onion till transparent. Put Kidney dice into lard with onions and sprinkle Paprika and salt over all. Cook for a few minutes to lightly brown Kidneys, add Bay leaves and mace. Add water to cover and slowly cook for 30 to 45 minutes. After 30 minutes, see if the kidney dice is tender, and cooked. If it is done, remove from heat. If it is too soft, continue cooking for another 15 minutes. You do not want the Kidney to get tough. Stir two tablespoons of flour into a cup with 2 Tbs. of soft butter. Make a roux by blending flour and butter till well mixed. Stir this into the Kidney stew, and let it cook till it is thickened. Remove bay leaves.

Serve Kidney Stew over cooked potatoes and a dollop of sour cream. Nice to have, chopped hot banana peppers to sprinkle over stew for spiciness.

Authentic Hungarian Plum Dumplings (Szilvas gomboc)

Plum Dumplings are a treat many people have never had. Plump potato dough surrounding a pitted plum juicy with sugar and cinnamon, and swimming in buttered bread crumbs. When you cut into them the purple juices run out like a garnet river. What flavor, what a meal. Yes, this is a meal. Some men have contests to see how many they can consume at a sitting. Thirty is not unheard of, though four is an usual serving. You can not eat just one. Some Hungarian mothers make them big with a lot of dough, others use less dough.

- 2 1/2 dz. free stone Italian plums, washed, split, pit removed
- 4 or 5 medium sized potatoes
- 1 egg beaten
- 4 cups of flour (unsifted)
- 1 tsp. salt
- buttered bread crumbs
- sugar
- cinnamon

Peel potatoes and cook in salted water till soft. Drain and peel.
Mash potatoes and add warm to sifted flour and salt on a kneading surface.
Make a well and add egg and knead gently till all is blended.
On a clean floured surface, roll dough out to 1/2 inch thick.
Cut dough into 4 inch squares and put a plum into center of each square.
Place 1/2 tsp. sugar and a sprinkle of cinnamon in the hole of the plum.
Fold corners to the middle and roll the dumpling in your hands till round.
Cook a few dumplings at a time in salted water for about 10 minutes.
Remove with a slotted spoon.

Place in a pan in which bread crumbs have been toasted in butter (one cup crumbs to 1/4 cup butter) and mixed with 1/2 cup of sugar and 2 tsp. cinnamon. Keep warm.
When all the dumplings have been cooked and are in the pan, gently spoon the bread crumbs, butter, sugar and cinnamon mix over all.

Serve warm with bread crumb topping and a dollop of Sour Cream if desired.

Authentic Hungarian Pork Roast with Onion Gravy, Caraway Sauerkraut and Dumplings from Aunt Violet

It took me 61 years to find out that this most loved and often made dish was not Hungarian but Bohemian. It was a legacy of my Godmother, Violet Zellner who was Bohemian and who's name I bore as June Violet. Aunt Vi had three sons and she loved to have me come for a visit to their home on the far south side of Chicago, miles from our home on the near north side. I would take the old red Halsted Street cars to the end of the line and then have to walk a block or two. She used to call me "Dolly" or "Sweetie Pie". She was the first person I knew who had an electric stove. I remember her serving this dish with a dumpling as huge as a loaf of bread.

- 1 large pork roast about 6 or 7 lbs. (If not lean, trim some fat)
- 7 large onions, peeled and chopped (do not lessen amount of onions, it s your gravy)
- 2 Tbs. sugar (do not omit, caramelizes the onions)
- salt and pepper

Sear all sides of roast in a hot roasting pan over high heat. Do not add any fat. (May set off smoke detectors). Put all the chopped onions and 2 Tbs. of sugar into roasting pan with meat and cover. Place in a medium heat 325 degree oven and slowly roast for about 1 1/2 to 2 hours. Check the roast periodically to turn it over and push the onions around. The onions should be taking on a rich brown color.

Caraway Sauerkraut

- 2 lbs. of sauerkraut, rinsed and drained (I like the pouched kind rather than canned).
- 1 cup of water
- 1 Tbs. of caraway seeds
- 1 Tbs. of sugar

- 2 Tbs. of lard or butter
- 2 Tbs. of flour

In the meantime, rinse the sauerkraut once with water, and put into a pot along with the Caraway seeds and tablespoon of sugar, and cup of water. Slowly cook till kraut is soft about 1/2 hour. When Kraut is soft, blend 2 Tbs. of butter or lard with 2 Tbs. of flour and stir into the Kraut mixing it in and stirring while the roux cooks to thicken the Kraut. Be sure it simmers a few minutes to cook away the raw flour. Keep warm.

Farina Dumplings

- 4 Tbs. soft butter
- 4 eggs
- Farina
- 1/2 teas. salt

Put a pot of water on to boil. Mix the soft butter, salt and the 4 eggs well. Add farina 1/4 cup at a time till you have a dumpling dough consistency. Thick, not runny. Then add a little water for moisture. When the water boils, cut the dumplings into the water with a tablespoon. When they come to the top, cook about 5 minutes more. Drain and arrange on meat platter. Keep warm. When the Pork Roast is finished, remove the roast to a board and carve it into slices. To the onions in the roasting pan add 2 cups of water into which 2 Tbs. of flour have been stirred.

While stirring the gravy use a spatula to "wash down" the caramelized meat and onion juices which have colored the sides of the roaster. This contains a lot of flavor and color for your Onion Gravy. Taste and adjust seasoning with salt. Serve dumplings on the meat platter with a few spoonfulls of gravy poured over. Caraway Sauerkraut is served in a side dish and the Onion Gravy is served in a gravy boat. Beer is the preferred drink. This is a feast fit for a Hungarian or Bohemian King. If you have left overs (which I doubt) this reheats nicely. If you have cooked too many dumplings, they can be frozen and used in soup or Gulyas.

Note: You can substitute Modern Potato Dumplings for the Farinna Dumplings if you prefer. (See Modern Potato Dumplings on page 57).

Potatoes and Dumplings with Breadcrumbs (Morzsaott krumpliss gomoc)

During the Great Depression I remember two dishes my Mother would make to feed our family during those lean years. One was KAISER'S SCHMARN and the other was Grundbarra Und Knoedel (Potatoes and Dumplings with Breadcrumbs).

The dumplings were the basic Farina Dumplings cooked in water, served with peeled and cooked cut up potatoes and then served with breadcrumbs that were sautéed in a lot of butter. Not a dish to serve up for someone on a diet, but in those Depression years dieting was not a concern.

We never went hungry, always went to bed with a full stomach. Potatoes and flour were always available and we always had a nice cooked fruit, like plums, peaches or a nice cucumber salad or cold slaw to eat with these meals. This dish still is a good lenten dish, or a respite from meat dishes.
It is surprisingly tasty.

We children never knew how hard it was for our parents to survive this era. We did notice the concern on our parents faces when our shoe soles were worn out before the shoes were paid for.

- 4 Tbl. butter
- 4 eggs
- Farina
- 1/2 teas. salt
- 4 med. sized potatoes
- 1 cup of good Italian bread crumbs
- 1 stick of butter for frying the breadcrumbs

Mix the 4 Tbl. butter, 1/2 salt and the 4 eggs well. Add farina 1/4 cup at a time till you have a dumpling dough consistency. Then add a little water for moisture. Put on a large pot of water to boil. Add the raw potatoes to the pot and cook till allmost done. Cut the dumplings into the water with a tablespoon. When they come to the top, cook about 5 minutes more. Drain potatoes and dumplings and toss into pan with fried breadcrumbs. Toss together so that breadcrumbs are evenly distributed. Adjust salt and pepper to taste. Good to serve with a cold Cucumber Salad with Sour Cream and a cooked fruit like peaches, plums, etc.

Serves 4.

Authentic Hungarian Roast Chicken or Turkey (Csirke-vagy pulykasult)

This is the one and only poultry stuffing my family has ever made. It is a wonderful Hungarian stuffing that has been in the family for 8 generations. I have never seen or tasted this dressing outside of my maternal family group. I only make roast chicken or turkey just to get the stuffing, which absorbs the juices of the bird while it roasts. This stuffing can not be made outside of the bird's cavity. It needs the close embrace of the bird to be succulent.

Amount for one 10 to 15 lb. Turkey (Halve recipe for a medium size chicken)

- 2 large loaves of sliced white bread
- one large onion
- 6 ribs of celery along with leaves
- 2 or 3 bunches or 2 cups or more of FLAT LEAF PARSLEY (Do not substitute curly)
- 1 1/2 sticks of butter
- 1 cup of water
- 4 whole raw eggs
- 2 tsp. salt
- 1/2 tsp. pepper
- 1/4 lbs. or one stick of butter for basting

Cut bread into cubes, put into large mixing bowl. Finely chop washed parsley and place in bowl with bread cubes. Dice 1 onion and sauté with 1 1/2 sticks of butter in frying pan till translucent. Slice or dice ribs of celery and celery leaves and sauté along with onions. Add 1 cup of cold water to onion, celery and butter mixture to cool it off. Add 1 tsp. salt and 1/2 tsp. pepper to bowl with bread and parsley. Add 3 (THREE) RAW EGGS to the bowl of bread and parsley, along with the onion and celery mixture and mix well with your hands. The mixed stuffing should be moist, if it is not, add the 4th egg. The stuffing should NOT be

hot when you stuff the poultry. Heavily salt the inside cavity of the bird.
Really PACK the stuffing well into the bird. Any stuffing that does not fit can be stuffed into the cavity formed by the skin over the breast when it is separated by your hand to form a pocket. Truss and roast your bird as you normally would. Slice the butter for basting into cubes and tuck butter under wings, into folds of legs, and lay butter on top of breast. Baste the bird with butter and juices cooking out. When bird is done roasting, you will be able to carve up bird and open the breast area to lift out the loaf of parsley stuffing and slice into portions. Don't forget to make a wonderful gravy with the juices. It is also good the next day cold from the refrigerator.

Gravy

Into the pan with all the juices and drippings, place 2 cups of cold water that has been mixed with 2 heaping tablespoons of flour. Stir over low heat while scraping down the wall of the roasting pan to capture the caramelized juices of the bird. I use a rubber spatula. These dark brown juices encrusted on the pan walls will give a most wonderful color and flavor. Nice to swirl into the gravy, 1 tablespoon of butter which will give a final finished touch.

Note: Do not worry about bits of stuffing that may have fallen off of the bird into the juices. It will enhance the home quality of the gravy.

Authentic Hungarian Sauerkraut and Pork (Szekelagulyas)

Long ago, people had to lay away food to see them through the winter. Every house in the "old country" had a root cellar in which they stored their winter supply of onions, apples, squash, potatos, carrots, parsley roots and cabbage heads. In the fall you could smell the shredded cabbage fermenting in several large 30 gallon stoneware containers. I remember my father and mother bending over a wooden board that was made to shred cabbage heads. After it was shredded it was packed in layers with salt in large stoneware containers. It was hard work, but that sauerkraut was eaten with gusto and left you with a feeling of well being.

Sauerkraut was not only cheap and plentiful, but it was full of vitamins that warded off illness. It was a mainstay of Austrian-Hungarian winter cuisine.

This dish is an unusual mingling of sauerkraut, tomato, pork, onion and sour cream along with that ever present Hungarian sweet paprika.

- 2 lbs. pork cubed
- 1 &1/2 lbs. sauerkraut, rinse and drained
- 2 white onions, chopped
- 2 Tbls. lard or oil (if meat is very lean)
- 2 Tbls. Hungarian sweet paprika (no generic please)
- 1 large can of crushed tomato (or fresh tomatos peeled and crushed)
- 1 Tbls. sugar
- 2 bay leaves
- 1 cup of water
- 1/2 pint of sour cream (no yogurt please)
- salt and pepper to taste

Brown the meat and onion (in lard or oil if needed) in a pot with lid. Add the paprika to the meat and onion mix, stir to mix in (do not burn). Put in the drained sauerkraut, crushed tomatos, bay leaves and sugar. Mix. Cover pot. Cook slowly for about one hour, or until meat is tender. Add the sour cream and stir it in. The aroma will make your mouthwater. Serve in soup plates, with good crusty bread, a meal fit for the Kaiser.

This serves 4 and freezes well.

Hungarian style Smoked Beef Tongue (Fustolt marhanyelv)

We ate many things in our family, I would learn later in life, that were not commonly eaten by most Chicagoans. We ate heads, feet, tails, innards like kidneys, livers, heart. We were not fond of sweetbreads, brains, or stomach.

We ate these things not because we were poor, but because they were part of our culinary heritage and they were good! These were the foods my ancestors thrived on for many generations, and we thrived on them also.

A large whole beef tongue sitting in a pot of boiling water was not a pretty sight to a young child. But when it was stripped of it's sandpapery covering and thinly sliced, we children overlooked what the tongue looked like before and relished every bite of those horseshoe shaped slices. Beef tongue is easy to prepare.

- 3 to 4 lbs. smoked beef tongue
- 1 Tbl. salt
- 1 or 2 bay leaves
- 1 large onion
- 3 whole cloves
- 1/4 tsp. whole pepper corns
- 1 whole peeled clove of garlic
- 1 rib of celery
- 1 carrot
- sprig of parsley

Soak a 3 or 4 pound smoked tongue overnight in cold water.
The next day, cover it with fresh cold water, a large onion stuck with 3 whole cloves, 1 or 2 bay leaf, the

peppercorns, and spray of parsley, 1 whole peeled clove of garlic, a carrot, and rib of celery.

Bring to a simmer and let it cook for 3 hours or until it feels tender. Let it cool so you can handle it, and peel off the course bumpy tongue covering. Kitchen shears is helpful here. You will have to trim off any of the veins and glands at the base of the tongue. It should now look presentable. Slice thinly on the Diagonal, so the slices have a small horseshoe shape. It can be eaten hot or cold. I like to serve it with cold Sour Cream and Horseradish Sauce or warm Tomato sauce (see sauces index). Boiled potatoes go very well, as do dumplings too. Enjoy!

Note: The broth from cooking the tongue can be used as a stock for dried bean or pea soup. Taste to be sure the flavor is not overwhelming. If it is too strong, use 1/2 stock and 1/2 water for soup.

Serves 8 to 12

Authentic Hungarian Smoked Butt in Brown Sugar (Fustolt sertesfar nyerscukorban)

Smoked butt made in the Austrian-Hungarian style is wonderful and economical eating. The butt is cooked in brown sugar water. I find that the smoked butt is small enough to last for a few meals. It usually weighs about 3 to 4 pounds, is not full of fat. If you have not tried a smoked butt, you will be in for a surprise. It has very good smoked ham flavor. It makes a wonderful "corned beef and cabbage" meal for Saint Patrick's Day, but cooks much faster than corned beef. Only 40 minutes a pound and it is done, versus hours for corned beef. No fatty waste.

- 1 smoked pork butt about 3 lbs.
- 3 Tbl. brown sugar
- 2 quarts of water

Place Butt in pot large enough to hold at least 2 quarts of water (enough to cover butt), add the brown sugar and simmer on top of stove in covered pot, 40 minutes to each pound of butt. When done, remove butt from pot but do not throw away cooking liquid. Slice and serve warm with boiled or mashed potatoes and vegetable. Sour Cream Coleslaw on the side is nice. The wonderfully flavored cooking water is used to make a delicious soup, with the addition of cabbage, tomato, onion, potatoes. (See Sweet and Sour Cabbage Soup recipe). Smoked butt is versatile and full of tender meat.

Authentic Hungarian Sticky Chicken (Uveg)

This is one of my favorite childhood meals. It is called Sticky Chicken because when you eat the chicken it sticks to your fingers. It is truly "finger licking good". It is a dish that even today, I can never get enough of. You just want to eat more and more.

This is a dish that originated in Serbia where it is called Uveg. It is made in a single pot, that is, never uncovered until it is done. Cook it low and long, you will be able to tell after about an hour when it is done purely by smell. It will smell delicious.

After an hour you can peek, watch out! The steam can burn you nose! The rice should be fully cooked and sticky along with the chicken.

- 1/2 cup lard
- 1 chicken cut up or the equivalent chicken parts, skin on. (Do not use boneless chicken)
- 1 large onion peeled and chopped
- 2 cups of raw white rice, washed in cold water and slightly drained
- 1 heaping Tbs. of Hungarian paprika
- 1 1/2 tsp. salt
- 1 small green or banana pepper chopped
- 1 bay leaf
- 1 1/2 cups water
- 6 peeled and seeded fresh tomatoes chopped **-OR-** 1 large can of whole tomatoes, not drained but pulled apart

I use a heavy black iron pot with a heavy lid. Put into pot 1/2 cup of lard and just brown all sides of chicken legs, wings, breasts, backs, etc. If you have liver and gizzards use them also. Remove chicken from pot and set aside. Into the juices and lard in the pot, saute 1 chopped onion along with the 2 cups of rinsed raw rice. Just saute rice and onion until onion is transparent. Stir in 1 heaping Tbs. of Hungarian Pakrika and 1 1/2 teas. of salt. Into pot, add 1 chopped green pepper, and one can of whole tomatoes that were not drained and pulled apart along with 1 1/2 cup of water. Add 1 bay leaf and mix up the rice and veggie mix. Now layer the browned chicken into the rice and veggie mix. I just scoop up some rice mix and lay chicken underneath, rice layer, chicken layer. Give the pot a shake to settle everything. Now start the pot to simmer on a moderate heat on top of the stove, when it all starts to cook, LOWER THE HEAT and put the cover on and DO NOT LIFT UP THE COVER FOR AT LEAST 60 MINUTES. You must slowly cook and give it a shake once in a while, but do not uncover. You will smell the wonderful aroma of cooked chicken when it is done. If you smell burning, your heat is too high. Use the lowest heat possible, you can hear if it is cooking. Adjust salt seasoning, this dish should not be sloppy like a stew, it should be moist. When I make it sometimes the rice sticks to the bottom of the pot, but it is good and chewy. I love this dish, can't eat enough of it.

Serve with a salad like Cucumber with Sour Cream, or Coleslaw to be Authentic. Or you can serve it with a nice green lettuce salad.

Serves 4 to 6.

Authentic Hungarian Stuffed Cabbage (Sorma or Toltottkaposzta)

Stuffed Cabbage or Sorma, is the National dish of Serbia. No wedding or funeral feast would be complete without large pots full of Sorma. Sorma consists of tightly rolled bundles of meat and rice held together by a soft wrappers of cabbage. The rolls are piled on a bed of silky sauerkraut. It is one of those dishes that once tasted, can never be forgotten. Cabbage and sauerkraut combine to make a mellow dish.

- 3/4 lb. ground pork (you can also make it with all ground beef).
- 3/4 lb. ground beef
- 1/2 lb. Hungarian sausage, (or you can use mild Pepperoni, it is close to the taste of Hungarian paprika sausage) sliced in 1 inch chunks (Sausages Optional)
- 2 raw eggs
- 2 tsp. salt
- 1 Tbl. paprika
- 1/2 tsp. pepper corns
- 3/4 lb. of rice
- 2 large bay leaves
- 2 white onions chopped
- 3 Tbl. shortening (use corn, peanut oil or lard).
- 1 large head of cabbage
- 1 bottle or pack of sauerkraut (Do not use canned), rinsed in cold water.

Brown the chopped onion in shortening, and place in mixing bowl with ground meats, raw eggs, uncooked rice, paprika, salt. Mix well with your clean hands. Take out the core of the cabbage. Leave head whole. Place in large pot of boiling water to wilt the outer leaves. You will be able to gently pull off whole cabbage leaves. Trim off thick center vein of cabbage leaves. Make a pile of leaves on your work station. You may want to shake excess water off. Place 2 Tbsp. of meat and rice mixture on a leaf (starting at the thick end) and roll it up and tuck in ends with your finger. Make as many as you can. Arrange the rolls in cooking pot. Put a few chunks of sausage here and there between the rolls. Cover the rolls two-thirds full of water, arrange rinsed sauerkraut on top, sprinkle over the peper corns and the bay leaves on top, COVER and cook slowly for about 1 1/2 hours, or until the rice is tender. Serve with good crusty bread and cold beer.

Serves 6.

Authentic Hungarian Stuffed Green Peppers (Toltottpaprika)

Stuffed Peppers was once a dish that was only made in the pepper and tomato growing season. Now we can enjoy this dish all year round. It makes a delectable meal. Slow, low cooking is the secret.

- 8 medium sized green peppers **OR** you can use 10 or 12 bannana peppers (hot or mild)
- 3/4 lb. ground beef **OR** 1 lb. beef if you do not want to include pork
- 3/4 lb. ground pork
- 1 raw egg
- 1 cup washed rice
- 2 28 oz. cans of crushed tomatos **OR** 3 or 4 lbs. fresh peeled tomatos
- 1 large white onion, chopped
- 2 Tbsp. good Hungarian paprika (buy imported sweet)
- 1 tsp. salt
- 2 Tbls. sugar (do not omit)
- 1/4 tsp. black pepper corns
- 2 whole bay leaves
- 1 cup water only if needed

Cut off the tops of peppers and reserve. Take out the seeds. In mixing bowl, place the ground meat, raw egg, washed rice, salt and paprika. Mix well with clean hands. Stuff peppers, using all the meat mixture. If you have some left over, make a few balls. Set peppers up-right in cooking pot. Add the tomatos, sugar, onions and chopped tops of peppers over the peppers, toss in the black pepper corns and the bay leaves. Cover and slowly cook for about 1 1/2 hours. If it looks too thick add a little water.

Serves 4.

Authentic Hungarian Wiener Schnitzel or Veal Cutlets (Becsiszelet)

We used to eat a lot of veal. Veal breast, stuffed with our family's special Parsley stuffing, sautéed Veal slices with slices of delicious kidney still attached, savory Szekely Goulash made with cubes of veal and pork, tomato and sour kraut. My favorite was Wiener Schnitzel. For me they conjured up images of beautiful people in 19th century Vienna swirling and waltzing to the music of Strauss. I heard stories of Vienna, of the beauty, the music, the fashions, the food, the bakeries from my mother and Aunt.

Wiener Schnitzel is not the extravagant dish people think it is today. Veal cutlets are expensive. But there is no waste, no bones, no fat. They are pounded very thin and coated with a delectable covering. A little goes a long way.

- 2 lbs. of veal cutlets trimmed of any sinew
- 1 or 2 whole beaten eggs
- 1/2 to 1 cup of flour
- 2 cups of fine white bread crumbs
- salt
- pepper
- 3 or 4 Tbls. butter **OR** lard
- 2 fresh lemons quartered

Beat or pound the veal cutlets until very thin. I use two thick pieces of plastic and a hammer.
Lightly salt and pepper the veal cutlets. Dip the pieces of veal into a dish of the flour, coat both sides and shake off the excess flour. The flour coating will help the egg coating to adhere. Dip the pieces of floured veal into the dish of the beaten raw egg and coat both sides Press the pieces of veal into a bowl of fine white bread crumbs. Coat both sides with crumbs.
Let the bread crumbed veal slices dry flat for at least 1/2 hour.

Heat the butter or lard in a large frying pan. I prefer lard. Lard has the advantage of not scorching as easily as butter and lard makes a tastier browned coating.

Sauté the cutlets until they are a golden brown. The thin cutlets will cook quickly, it will not take long. Perhaps 4 min. on each side. You will know when to turn it over, the bottom breading will be a golden brown.

Do not cover finished cutlets with a cover. The steam will soften the bread crumb coating and it will fall off.

Serve topped with quarters of lemon. The lemon juice is squeezed on the cutlet according to preference.

Note: Leftover cutlets are delicious cold with a mayonnaise dressing, and can be reheated for a cutlet sandwich. You can also use pounded chicken breast instead of veal for chicken schnitzel.

Serves 4 to 6.

Authentic Hungarian Green Beans with Dill (Kapros zoldbabfozelek)

Hungarian style green beans are unusual in that it combines, beans, onions, fresh dill, vinegar and sugar to make a dish that is sweet, sour, and dilly. This could only come from Hungary, where variety of taste in a meal is commonplace. Use fresh or frozen cut green beans for this dish. Not canned! It has always been received by non-Hungarians as a new and delicious taste sensation.

- 2 packages of green beans
- 2 Tbl. lard or butter
- 2 Tbl. flour
- 1/2 cup of sliced onion
- 1/4 cup of good vinegar
- 2 tsp. sugar
- 1 Tbl. chopped dill

Cook beans in salted water till tender, not soft. Melt lard or butter, add onions and saut till limp, add chopped dill. Then add flour making a roux. Add 1 cup of water, sugar and vinegar and stir while the sauce gets thick. Add drained beans, and mix, if too thick add a little more water.

Serves 4 to 6.

Authentic Hungarian Style Cauliflower or Broccoli (Magyaros karfiol vagy brakoli)

We always had a copious amount of homemade breadcrumbs made from the bread that was baked in a large turkey roaster. The dried bread was stored in a paper bag in the oven. When ever we needed crumbs for Apple Strudel, fried chicken, Wiener Schnitzel, Hungarian Hamburgers, cauliflower or broccoli we would grate the hard bread on the side of the grater to make as much as we needed. The best crumbs are the kind you make your self from good white bread. The crumbs should be large, not ground to a sand like texture. Cauliflower or broccoli was served in this simple but very flavorful way.

Hungarian Style Cauliflower

Cook a whole head of cauliflower in a pot of salted water till tender. Drain and place whole head on a serving dish. In a saute pan melt 1/4 lb. butter and medium brown 1 cup of bread crumbs, season with 1/8 tsp. salt. Stir and toss crumbs. Do not let it burn or it will be bitter. Spoon butter and crumb mixture over the top of cauliflower and serve. Mmmmmm! Serves 4 to 6

Hungarian Style Broccoli

Substitute broccoli in place of cauliflower. Trim off thick stems of broccoli. You can keep the broccoli in one head or break it into flowerets. Cook in salted water till tender. Drain and place on a serving dish. In a saute pan melt 1/4 lb. butter and medium brown 1 cup of bread crumbs, season with 1/8 tsp. salt. Stir and toss crumbs. Do not let it burn or it will be bitter. Spoon butter and crumb mixture over the top of broccoli and serve. Mmmmmm!

Serves 4 to 6

Authentic Hungarian Style Mashed Potatoes (Magyaros tojasos krumplipure)

The lowly potato is often served at every Hungarian meal. It helped stretch the Goulyas and it was an important ingredient in many dumplings, soups, breads. Mashed potatoes made with real butter and sour cream and egg is usually a Sunday dinner treat. A gardening hint for those of you who plant potatoes. "Do not plant potatoes so deep that they can't hear the church bells" (Old Hungarian proverb).

- 8 to 10 potatoes peeled and quartered
- 1/4 lb. of butter or 1 stick
- 1/2 cup of sour cream
- 1 raw egg
- salt to taste

Boil peeled and quartered potatoes in salted water till tender. Strain off cooking water. Add butter to pot and mash potatoes. Add 1/2 of sour cream, blend in potatoes. Add 1 whole raw egg into potato mixture and whip. Add a little more sour cream if not moist enough. Add salt to taste. These Mashed Potatoes Hungarian Style can be reheated and they will hold their creamy and moist taste. They will not get hard and pasty.

Serves 6 to 8.

Authentic Hungarian Style Spinach (Magyaros spenotfozelek)

I never knew what spinach was until I was a teenager. My parents always planted Swiss chard, with the red veins, because the yield was greater than spinach and the flavor was milder. I remember picking the Swiss chard and washing those giant leaves for Hungarian creamed Swiss chard or spinach. This is creamed spinach with a Transylvanian touch.

- 1 lb. of fresh spinach or swiss chard, cooked, well drained and chopped **OR** 1 pack of frozen chopped spinach, thaw, cook and drain well
- 2 Tbs. butter
- 1 clove of fresh garlic, finely chopped
- 2 Tbs. flour
- 1/4 tsp. salt
- 1/8 tsp. ground pepper
- 3/4 cup of cream **OR** milk

Melt in a small saucepan over low heat 2 Tbs. butter with 1 finely chopped fresh garlic clove. Saute garlic in butter a minute or so. Do not let garlic burn or it will be bitter. Blend in 2 Tablespoons flour to make a roux. Add 1/4 tsp. salt, 1/8 tsp. pepper and heat until mixture bubbles, stirring constantly. Remove from heat. Add gradually 3/4 cup of cream or milk. Return to heat and stir until mixture is smooth and thickened. Blend well drained spinach into sauce and serve.

Serves 4.

Authentic Hungarian Hot Paprika, Tomato, Onion and Pepper Condiment (Lecso)

Lesco can be any thing you want it to be. It is very versatile. A cooked mixture of onions, yellow banana peppers, and tomatoes and paprika. Add some sliced Hungarian Sausage and it can be served as an appetizer or stew. Serve it over dumplings or rice as a main course. Spoon it over scrambled eggs for breakfast. Use it as a sauce for sausage or corn meal mush. However you use it you will find it to be quite compatible with a lot of dishes. It is an ancient dish originating in Serbia.

- 2 Tbs. lard or oil
- 2 med. onions sliced
- 1 lb. of yellow sweet banana peppers, seeded and sliced. Do not use green bell peppers they have no flavor and will turn to pulp.
- 3 large, very ripe tomatoes, peeled and diced. (If you cannot get good tomatoes you can use canned tomatoes if you drain them well)
- 1/2 Tbs. sugar
- 1/2 Tbs. salt
- 1 Tbs. paprika

Heat lard, add sliced onion, and cook over very low heat for 5 minutes. Add green pepper slices and cook for an additional 15 min. Add tomatoes, sugar, salt and paprika. Cook for 10 to 15 min. longer. Adjust sugar and salt to taste. If you are going to put sausage into it, reduce salt.

Toward the end of the summer grownig season, I make a large batch of Lecso and ladle it into pint size containers for storage in the freezer. I use it all winter long. It is excellent as a sauce base for chicken, pork, beef, sausage, eggs, rice, noodles, potatoes, pasta and vegetables.

Authentic Hungarian Parsley Stuffing for Chicken, Turkey or Veal

This recipe is generations old. It was the only stuffing we ever used and I think it is the best I have ever tasted. My Heirloom Stuffing is filled with chopped fresh parsley. It is the primary flavor, along with celery, onion, butter. The texture is firm, like a meat loaf and is cut in slices. The women in the family would compete with one another to make the most tasty and best stuffing. This is not for any one who is counting calories. This stuffing imparts the best flavor to chicken, turkey or veal. I am sure that once you taste this dressing it will become a favorite of yours.

- 1 large loaf of sliced white bread or 2 small loaves
- 1 onion
- 6 ribs of celery along with leaves
- 2 or 3 bunches or 2 cups or more of FLAT LEAF PARSLEY (Do not substitute curley)
- 1 1/2 sticks of butter
- 1 cup of water
- 4 whole raw eggs
- 2 tsp. salt
- 1/2 tsp. pepper

Cut bread into cubes, put into large mixing bowl. Finely chop washed parsley and place in bowl with bread cubes. Dice 1 onion and saute with butter in frying pan till translucent. Slice or dice ribs of celery and celery leaves and saute along with onions. Add 1 cup of cold water to onion, celery and butter mixture to cool it off. Add 1 tsp. salt and 1/2 tsp pepper to bowl with bread and parsley. Add 4 raw eggs to the bowl of bread and parsley, along with the onion and celery mixture and mix well with your hands. The stuffing should NOT be hot when you stuff the poultry. Really PACK the stuffing well into the bird. Any stuffing that does not fit can be stuffed into the cavity formed by the skin over the breast when it is separated by your hand to form a pocket. Roast your bird as you normaly would. Baste the bird with butter and juices cooking out.

When bird is done roasting, you should be able to carve up bird and open the breast area to lift out the loaf of parsley stuffing and slice into portions. Don't forget to make a wonderful gravy with the juices.

It is also good the next day cold from the refrigerator.

Enough for a small turkey or big Chicken.

Authentic Hungarian Potato Cakes (Langos or Krumplislangos)

During the long winters when Hungarians needed substantial snacks to keep their bodies fueled, a potato dough fried in Lard was a good choice. The smell is heavenly, they are smeared with the juice of a cut garlic clove and eaten warm. We children would stand impatiently around the kitchen waiting to get the first cakes out of the pan. In Hungarian kitchens the mother would feed the children and men first and then she served herself last.

- 3 or 4 med. potatoes
- 1/2 envelope of dry yeast
- 1/2 cup of warm milk for yeast
- 1/2 tsp. sugar
- 1 1/2 cups to 1 2/3 cups of flour
- 1/2 tsp. salt
- lard for frying

Cook the potatoes in boiling salted water. Peel them and immediately mash them. You should have about 1 1/2 cups. Cool. Mix the warm milk with the yeast and sugar. Let the starter sit for 5 or 10 minutes. Mix mashed potatoes with flour and the salt. Start with 1 1/2 cups and add more flour to make a kneadable dough. Knead dough well. Put dough in a bowl and cover. Let dough rise in a warm place until double in bulk. About 1 hour. Roll out the dough with a floured rolling pin on a floured board to 1/2 inch thick. Cut into rectangles, squares or circles. Prick with a knife to keep big bubbles from forming. Melt Lard in a frying pan so it is at least 1/2 deep. Fry Langos over medium heat. If the lard is too hot they will burn, if the lard is to cool the Langos will absorb too much lard. You will have to watch them. Let them get a nice color. When they are done, rub each Langos with a cut clove of garlic and sprinkle with salt and Paprika.

Serve warm with sour cream. Good to accompany Bean or Lentil Soups, or a snack with beer or wine.

Authentic Hungarian Sweet and Sour Red Cabbage (Edes-savanyu voroskaposzta)

There is no food as colorful or as good as Cooked Red Cabbage made with lemon and brown sugar. Piles of shredded cabbage magically turn from dark purple to bright scarlet red. Red cabbage is similar to green cabbage, yet it has a different flavor that is hard to describe. I think red cabbage has a more intense flavor. Green cabbage is more delicate and nutty in flavor.

- 1 head of red cabbage
- 1/2 cup of diced smoked Hungarian bacon (can omit bacon if you double butter)
- 1/2 stick of butter (4Tbls.)
- 1 onion, diced
- 1 tsp. salt
- 1 apple grated
- 1 lemon
- 3 or 4 Tbls. brown sugar

Render the bacon, and remove the bacon or it will get too crisp and burn.
Add to pan with bacon fat, 1/2 stick of butter.
Sauté one med. onion in the bacon/butter fat until glossy.
Chop or shred a red cabbage and sauté in pan with onion and bacon fat, till somewhat limp. Do not let it burn. The large pile of cabbage will cook down to a third of the original amount. Do not be alarmed at the amount before cooking.
Sprinkle teaspoon salt over cabbage and onion.
Add to pan a large grated peeled and cored apple, the juice of a whole lemon and throw the reamed shell of lemon, cut into quarters, into the pan.
Add the cooked bacon dice or slices and stir in.
Cover and cook slowly till the red cabbage is tender, around 15 to 20 minutes. If it is too juicy, let it cook

without the cover.
Stir in about 3 or 4 tablespoons of Brown sugar to taste, depending on how sweet and sour you want it. Add more if desired. add ground pepper and more salt if desired.

Note: Red Cabbage is always better the second day. You can make it a day ahead of time to let it mellow.

Serves 6 to 8.

Authentic Hungarian Zucchini Squash with Dill (Teifeles tokkaposzta)

Summer meant zucchini squash canning season. Zucchini grown as big as a small watermelon. Bunches of fresh dill would be hanging in the summer kitchen waiting to be stuffed into the canning jars along with the noodled zucchini and vinegar. I never knew what fresh zucchini tasted like until I was a grown woman. Our zucchini was always pickled with dill to see us through the winter months. Remember, I am talking about 50 years ago. The only way we served zucchini was canned with dill and vinegar and then cooked with onion and sour cream. It looked like translucent noodles in a creamy white sauce. There is no way to compare the taste to anything similar. It is very distinctive. We had it often and loved it.

Today, it is impossible to buy giant zucchini. This recipe omits the canning process for an overnite brine soaking in the refrigerator. You will find it easy and very good.

- 6 zucchini squash (6-8" long or about 2 1/2 lbs.)
- 1 heaping Tablespoon of salt
- 1/2 cup good white vinegar
- a few sprigs of fresh dill
- 1 onion, 2" diameter, sliced

Wash and peel zucchini. Cut ends off and slice on a grater with large holes. Place zucchini noodles in a bowl, add 1 heaping Tbls. salt, 1/2 cup of vinegar and the dill. Mix well, cover and refrigerate overnite. When you are ready to prepare it, transfer squash to a cooking pot, and add enough water to just come to the top of the squash. Don't drown it! Add the sliced onion, mix well and cook. You can tell it is done when the squash changes color and takes on a creamy color. Pour off the brine, but do not throw it away as you may need some of it.

AFTER THE SQUASH IS COOKED

- 1/2 cup of sour cream
- 1 heaping Tbls. Flour
- 1 3/4 Tbls. sugar

In a small separate bowl, put 1/2 cup of sour cream plus 1 Tbls. flour and mix well. Add to hot drained squash stirring vigorously so you won't have any lumps. If it is too thick thin it out by adding 1 Tbls. of sour cream at a time alternating with the brine 1 Tbls. at a time. Then add your sugar and pick out the dill and serve. I hope this becomes a family favorite.

Note: I buy squash when it gets BIG (6 lbs. or more each) from a friendly farmer. A good test for whether the zucchini is past it's prime (too old) is to scrape the peel with your fingernail. If you can not scrape to the white easily, the squash is too old and hard. I will then process 12 to 15 pounds by cooking it in the brine with onions and dill. I then pack in freezer containers and freeze till needed. I then thaw, heat, drain brine, add sour cream, flour and sugar and enjoy!

Serves 4 to 6.

Hungarian Dill Sauce for Meat or Poultry (Kapormartas hushov vagy szarnyashoz)

Dill grows wild in most Hungarian gardens. Year after year it keeps reseeding itself. It grows to great heights. Cool green lacey fronds, pungent with the familiar aroma, waiting to be stripped for sauces and salads. Mature plants top heavy with seed heads will be hung upside down in the canning kitchen to dry for squash and pickles. This dill sauce has a creamed base, is sweet-sour and served hot over boiled beef and vegetables after the HUNGARIAN BEEF SOUP has been consumed. Also serve hot over boiled chicken after the HUNGARIAN CHICKEN SOUP has been consumed.

- 1 1/2 Tbls. soft butter
- 1 1/2 Tbls. flour
- 1 cup of milk or water or stock
- 1 1/2 tsp. good vinegar
- 1/2 tsp. sugar
- 1 tsp. fresh dill chopped
- 1/8 tsp. salt

You are going to make a basic cream sauce. Start by melting the butter in a saucepan. Sprinkle the flour over the butter, stir and cook until the mixture foams up. Do not let it brown. Stir in the milk, water or stock and cook stirring so no lumps form. When thickened, stir in vinegar, sugar, fresh dill and salt. Taste and adjust seasoning if needed.

Makes over 1 cup.

This recipe can be doubled or trippled if more is needed.

Hungarian Sour Cream and Horse-Radish Sauce (Tejfeles tormamartas)

Sour cream is a staple in a hungarian kitchen. Practically every meal has something made with sour cream, soup, salad, goulash, pancakes, vegetables, desserts and sauces. This simple sauce is a mainstay when ever we have hungarian sausage, or boiled beef.

- 2 cups of sour cream
- 4 Tbls. prepared grated horse-radish
- 2 tsp. sugar
- 1/2 tsp. salt

Mix together in small sauce bowl. Add more horse-radish if you like it stonger, more sour cream and sugar if you like it milder. Serve at room temperature with boiled beef from HUNGARIAN BEEF SOUP recipe or with boiled chicken from HUNGARIAN CHICKEN SOUP recipe or with HUNGARIAN SAUSAGE.

Makes 2 cups.

Authentic Hungarian Tomato Sauce (Paradicsommartas)

A cooked creamy tomato sauce that is very unlike a tomato spaghetti sauce. This tomato sauce is traditionally served over boiled beef and vegetables, after having consumed the beef soup. It is also traditionally served over boiled chicken, after having consumed the chicken soup.

- 1 1/2 Tbls. soft butter
- 1 1/2 Tbls. flour
- 1 cup of water or stock
- 1 heaping Tbls. tomato paste
- 1/2 tsp. sugar
- 1/8 tsp. salt
- 2 tsp. vinegar

You are going to make a basic white sauce. Melt the butter in a saucepan. Sprinkle the flour over the butter, stir and cook until the mixture foams up. Do not let it brown. Stir in the tomato paste, water or stock and cook stirring so no lumps form. When thickened, stir in sugar, and salt. Taste and adjust seasoning if needed. If you like more "bite" you can add 1 tsp. of vinegar. Makes over 1 cup of sauce. Recipe can be doubled or tripled if more is needed.

Serve hot over boiled beef and vegetables in HUNGARIAN BEEF SOUP or serve hot over boiled chicken in HUNGARIAN CHICKEN SOUP.

You can also add a tsp. of chopped fresh Dill for a Dill Tomato Sauce.

Authentic Hungarian Apple Strudel (Almasretes)

Special occasions meant Apple Strudel time. As Christmas and Thanksgiving fall in winter when apples were at their best, Apple Strudel was then always served. When my Grandma made strudel, she would have all hands available helping. The dining room table would be covered with a white cloth on which the strudel dough would be pulled thin until you could read a newspaper through it. The women would walk around the table stretching the dough by lifting it with their round knuckles to avoid tears. When all the apple slices and ingredients were spread out on the tissue dough, the eldest would supervise the rolling up of the strudel by pulling up on the cloth to create a big roll of strudel. When the rolling was done, the roll would be cut into 6 or 8 sections, the ends tucked under and all placed into the oven to bake. When the strudel was done, we children would fight to get the thick juice that cooked out onto the pan. It was like candy, apple, cinnamon, and butter flavor all mixed together. Today we can get apples all year round and purchased Filo dough saves a lot of back breaking work.

Here is a simple way of making good Hungarian strudel. Buy FILO dough. You will be able to find it where the frozen pastry shells are. It is as good as homemade but much less work. Follow directions for strudel, using melted butter to brush on filo tissue.

- 1 package of Filo dough
- 1 and 1/2 sticks of butter, melted
- 2 lbs. apples, peeled, cored, and sliced thin
- 1 tsp.cinnamon
- 1 cup sugar
- 1 cup of toasted breadcrumbs
- 1 large clean kitchen towel (used to roll strudel)

Mix apples with crumbs (crumbs help to keep juice in strudel instead of flooding pan). Mix suger and cinnamon in a dish. Lay out clean towel and put sheets of buttered Filo dough on top. Place apples on prepared filo layers that have been brushed with butter. Start spreading apples about 3 inches from the edge closest to you, you need a clean area so you can get it in the pan. Completly cover the rest of the filo dough with apples. Sprinkle cinnamon and sugar mix over the apples. Now take the edge of the towel near you and slowly start to make a big roll by pulling up and towards you. This is not as hard as it sounds. As you are rolling it you can roll it right into a greased pan. Then tuck the ends of the strudel underneath itself. Brush top with more butter and bake at 350 degrees for about 1 hour. Brush every 20 min. with butter. Strudel is done when it looks like it has collapsed. Cool and cut into slices and dust with powderd sugar. You can vary the filling by adding chopped walnuts, or raisins. If you add raisins you must first soften them in hot water and then dry them before using. I prefer using just apples. When you lay out the filo sheets you will want to have at least 4 or 6 layers buttered one on top of the other. You will have enough sheets to make several strudels so buy at least 4 or 5 lbs of apples. It is not really a lot of work and you will have a wonderful dessert.

Authentic Hungarian Bismarck Doughnuts from Grandma Sehne (Fank)

Grandma Sehne (Elizabeth Heinz) was my Mother's Mother and made these wonderful Hungarian Bismarck Doughnuts. Prince Otto von Bismarck was the Chancellor of Germany from 1871 to 1890. These filled doughnuts were named after him. We children loved to eat them warm from the pot, covered in powdered sugar. Sometimes Grandma made them with a hole in the middle, and sometimes without so they could be filled with Rasberry Jam. I still have the old metal pastry syringe that she brought from Hungary to pump in the jam. My brother used to chase me around the kitchen teasing me with it as though he was going to give me an injection of red jelly.

- 4 cups of flour
- 1 1/2 cups milk
- 2 pk. yeast
- 4 heaping Tbl. sugar
- a dash of salt
- 4 Tbl. butter
- 8 egg yolks

Boil milk, add butter and sugar, and then cool. Add yeast and milk and beat egg yolks in well with beater. Add this mixture to flour. Let rise for 2 hours. Roll out lighly on floured board to 3/8 inch thickness, and cut out round circles. Lighly cover with cloth and let rise again about 1/2 hour. Fry in hot Crisco oil (Vegetable oil) or Lard. Bismarcks will turn nice brown on both sides after being flipped over. Bismarcks should drain for a few seconds on paper toweling. If you want Jelly Bismarcks, add Jelly after they are fried. Use a pastry bag to add jelly. You can also sprinkle powdered sugar on top of Bismarcks.

Authentic Hungarian Coffee Cake (Aranygaluska)

This coffee cake consists of balls of coffee cake dough made in a round tube cake-pan with nuts, cinnamon and a syrup-like glaze on the outside. This recipe is not a quick one. It uses yeast in the dough and that means a 2 1/2 to 3 hours spent in raising the dough. It is a good recipe for a lazy Saturday or Sunday. I always double the recipe to make two. One for the freezer and one for afternoon coffee.

- 10 inch tube pan
- 1 cup of sour cream
- 1/2 cup melted butter (no margarine)
- 1/2 cup sugar
- 1 tsp. salt
- 2 cakes yeast
- 3 eggs
- 4 1/2 cups of flour

Mixture to roll dough in

- 1/2 cup of soft butter melted
- 1 cup chopped walnuts
- 1 cup sugar
- 1 tsp. cinnamon

Mix sour cream, sugar, salt and yeast. Stir until yeast dissolves. Add eggs, softened butter and half the flour. Mix well and add rest of flour. Turn dough out on floured board and knead until smooth for about 10 to 15 minutes. Place in greased bowl. Cover and let rise in warm place until double in bulk for about 1 1/2 to 2 hours. Punch dough down. Turn over and let rise again for 45 minutes. After second rising, form into walnut-sized balls. Melt butter in small cup. Dip each ball in melted butter and roll in sugar and walnut and cinnamon mixture. Place in layers in 10-inch greased tube pan. Sprinkle any remaining sugar-nut mixture or melted butter over the top layer of balls. Cover pan with waxed paper and towel and let dough rise again 45 minutes. Bake 40 to 50 minutes at 375 degrees or until golden brown. Run spatula around sides of coffee cake, and invert onto plate.

To serve, break coffee cake apart with two forks.

Authentic Hungarian Apple Cake (Almaslepeny)

In the old days every season had it's bounty of produce. Fall and winter was the time to bake wonderful Apple Kuchen to go with the Hungarian coffee made with eggs. My Mother and her sister, Tante Betty, would linger over cups of coffee while debating the superiority of one type of apple over another. Today, we are fortunate that we have many varieties of apples from all over the world, accessible to us through out the whole year.

- 3 cups flour
- 1/4 cup of warm water
- 1 pkg. of yeast or 2 1/2 tsp. granulated yeast
- 1/2 stick of butter
- 3/4 cup scalded milk
- 3 Tbl sugar
- 1/4 tsp salt
- 4 egg yolks
- 3 to 4 lbs. of baking apples, washed, peeled, cored and thinly sliced (An apple peeler, corer and slicer is a wonderful tool to have)

Heat milk to scalding, then add butter and 1 1/2 Tbs of sugar, stir well until butter and sugar are dissolved. In small bowl, add yeast to water, with the other 1 1/2 Tbl. of sugar. Put 2 cups of flour in large bowl and add cooled milk, yeast mixture, eggs and salt. Beat well. Add the additional flour and work until dough comes away from sides of the bowl. Dough should be very soft and sticky. (If too thick, add a few teaspoons of warm water). Cover and let rise till double in bulk. This recipe will make 3 nine inch cake pans of Kuchen. When dough is ready, grease pan generously with butter, do not flour. Put a third of the dough in each pan, butter your hands, (otherwise the dough will stick to your hands). Using your fingers push dough to outer edges of pan, the dough will not want to stay there, but as you push apple slices down into the dough diagonally and over lapping like tiles on a roof, it will remain in place. Arrange the apple slices in a concentric spiral close together. Sprinkle each Kuchen with a third of the topping and dot with butter. (about 1/3 cup each).

Topping

- 1 cup sugar
- 2 heaping Tbl. flour
- 1 1/2 Tbl. cinnamon

Mix and sift ingredients together twice. Let rise for another 1/2 hour. Bake at 350 degrees for 35 to 45 minute or until sides and bottom are golden brown and apple slices are tender. Do not let it burn. We often double this recipe and make 6 or more. They freeze well and are nice to share.

Note: I cheat and take advantage of my bread machine to make the cake dough. It does all the kneading and proofing of the dough. I do not notice any difference from the hand kneading.

Makes 3 cakes.

Authentic Hungarian Pancakes (Palacsinta)

Heavenly thin and silky crepes spread with strawberry jam, rolled up and dusted with powdered sugar. Oh how we loved to hear that we were going to have Hungarian Tomato Soup! That meant Palacsinta with strawberry Jam for dessert. We always ate the two dishes together.

- 4 whole eggs
- 2 cups milk
- 2 tsp. sugar
- 1/2 tsp. salt
- 2 cups sifted flour
- butter

Mix flour, salt and sugar. Combine well beaten eggs and milk. Add egg and milk gradually to flour mixture, beating to a thin smooth batter. Let batter sit for 1/2 hour. This gets rid of the raw flour taste.
Spoon 3 Tbls. on hot buttered skillet. Will be very thin. Tilt skillet quickly in a circular motion to distribute batter over skillet. Brown lightly on both sides. Continue this until batter is used up.
As each crepe is done, spread with strawberry jam, roll up lightly and sprinkle with powdered sugar. These can be made ahead of time and reheated in a slow oven for a few minutes. You can also serve crepes with a dollop of sour cream.

Serves 4 to 6.

Authentic Hungarian Pecan and Butter Pretzel from Tante Miller

Tante Miller was born Barbara Sehne in Austria-Hungary. She was my grandfather's sister. My Great Aunt. She died in the 1950's when she was in her late seventy's. This was her recipe and until she died, it was made only by her. I am happy to share it with you. She was a wonderful cook and made this Butter Pretzel for every special occasion. It was a really a wonderful cake. It is full of butter, a lot of butter, and sprinkled with Pecan bits and finished off with an Almond icing. Do not be alarmed by the length of the recipe. It is not difficult. Once you have made this Butter Pretzel it will become a favorite of yours for special occasions. It is rich, but for special occasions......not too rich. It looks like a braid, but was called a Pretzel!

- 1/2 lb. butter room temp.
- 1 lb. chilled butter **OR** 4 more sticks chilled butter
- 1 cup sugar
- 2 whole eggs
- 2 cups of warm milk
- 1/4 tsp. ground nutmeg
- 1/2 tsp. ground cardamon
- 1/2 tsp. salt
- 7 cup of flour
- 2 packs dry yeast
- 1/2 cup warm water
- 1 tsp. sugar

In cup, mix yeast, 1/2 cup warm water and 1 tsp. sugar and let yeast develop. Cream 1/2 lb. butter or 2 sticks butter, sugar, eggs in mixing bowl. Add warm milk and yeast mixture and beat well. Add 6 cups of flour along with the salt, nutmeg and Cardamon till you have a soft dough. If it is too sticky, add the last cup of flour. Knead for 5 minutes. Cover and put in a warm place till double in size. Divide dough into 4 sections. One for each Pretzel. Take one section of dough and divide it into 3 equal strips. On floured surface stretch each strip of dough lengthwise to about 15 inches. Use fingers to do so. DO NOT USE ROLLING PIN. Take one stick or 1/4 lb. chilled butter and cut stick into 8 or 10 long narrow slivers of cold butter. Lay these slivers of butter on top of each of the three dough strips, about 3 slivers to a strip. Use up all the butter in the stick. Using fingers, enclose the slivers of butter by wraping the dough over the slivers. The object is to seal the butter in the strips. Now BRAID the 3 strips with the butter enclosed. Do it gently and keep it loose. Put the braided Pretzel into a circle in an ungreased pan. Sprinkle over the top of Pretzel at least 1/4 of a cup of coarse chopped Pecans. Bake at 350 degree oven for 30-35 minutes or until light brown. Do not let the pecans burn.

While Pretzel is still warm, drizzle over Almond sugar icing. Continue with the other 3 sections of dough to make 3 more Pretzels.

Topping for Butter Pretzel

- 1 1/2 cups of coarse chopped pecans, prefered
- 2 cups of powdered sugar, sifted
- 1/2 tsp. of pure almond extract
- 2 tsp. of water

Mix 2 cups of powdered sugar with 1/2 tsp. of Almond extract and 2 tsp. of water. Mix well, should not have any lumps. If this icing is too thick to drizzle over the Pretzels, thin with a little more water.

Makes 4 Pretzels.

Authentic Hungarian Plum Cakes (Szlivaslepeny)

I remember my Mother and I often sitting in the kitchen with bowls of purple plums in our laps, splitting the plums in half and removing the pits. The pans of "Kuchen" dough were waiting for the spirals of plum halves and coating of cinnamon and sugar. I always enjoyed pressing the plump plums into the dough, peel side down, and marveling at the beauty of the Plum cakes when they come out of the oven full of purple and scarlet juices, tart and sweet, as only plum Kuchen can be.

The purple plums best to use are the freestone Italian plums. If you haveever tried to cut out the pits from any other you will understand why. I always split a plum in the store to be sure that it is a freestone. When I bake, I will make 2 or 4 cakes to share with family. It is no more work to make several than one.

No bakery or store bought plum cake, no matter how beautiful it looks, can ever compete with a fresh home baked and warm from the oven, Hungarian Plum Cake. This cake is beautiful to see, the rich purple color of the plums develop and glaze with the sugar and cinnamon while baking.

- 3 cups flour
- 1/4 cup of warm water
- 1 pkg. of yeast or 2 1/2 tsp. granulated yeast
- 1/2 stick of butter
- 3/4 cup scalded milk
- 3 Tbl sugar
- 1/4 tsp salt
- 4 egg yolks
- 3 to 4 lbs. of Italian freestone plums, washed, cut in half and stoned

Heat milk to scalding, then add butter and 1 1/2 Tbs of sugar, stir well until butter and sugar are dissolved.

In small bowl, add yeast to water, with the other 1 1/2 Tbl. of sugar. Put 2 cups of flour in large bowl and add cooled milk, yeast mixture, eggs and salt. Beat well. Add the additional flour and work until dough comes away from sides of the bowl. Dough should be very soft and sticky. (If too thick, add a few teaspoons of warm water). Cover and let rise till double in bulk. This recipe will make 3 nine inch cake pans of Kuchen. When dough is ready, grease pan generously with butter, do not flour. Put a third of the dough in each pan, butter your hands, (otherwise the dough will stick to your hands). Using your fingers push dough to outer edges of pan, the dough will not want to stay there, but as you push plums skin side down into the dough, it will remain in place. Arrange the plums halves in a concentric spiral close together. Sprinkle each Kuchen with a third of the topping and dot with butter.

Topping

- 1 cup sugar
- 2 heaping Tbl. flour
- 1 1/2 Tbl. cinnamon
- 3/4 cup of butter (1/4 for each cake) to dot topping with.

Mix and sift sugar, flour and cinnamon together twice. Let rise for another 1/2 hour. Bake at 350 degrees for 30 to 35 minute or until sides and bottom are golden brown. We often double this recipe and make 6 or more. They freeze well and are nice to share.

Note: Use cake pans that are large enough for the dough to rise a little in, or you will have butter and sugar bubbling onto the rack and oven.

Makes 3 cakes.

Authentic Hungarian Poppy Seed Moon Strudel (Makosbeigli)

Here is a recipe for Poppy Seed Moon Strudel. I learned to make it from my grandmother and mother who were from Austria-Hungary. Every family has its own version of Mond Kuchen. These Strudels predate Christianity as the poppy was dedicated to the Moon goddess. Opium-sleep. The seeds are still called "Moon seeds" in german. The recipes are handed down by the women. The Moon Strudels are now usually made around Christmas time when all the fancy baking is done.

Poppy seeds can be purchase in bulk from a German Deli that specializes in imported spices. They should finely grind the seeds for you. You can also grind your own seeds in a coffee grinder. Grind the seeds well. It will make a big difference in the texture. You should not use the poppy seeds that come in small jars. They would be too expensive and not fresh enough. These Strudels can be wrapped in foil and stored in the freezer after they are baked. Hope you enjoy this Strudel.

Cake Dough

- 4 cups flour
- 4 Tablespoon sugar
- 1 cup lukewarm water
- 2 eggs slightly beaten
- 2 cakes yeast reg. or dry
- 1/2 cup soft butter
- 1 teaspoon salt

Crumble yeast in bowl, add water and sugar stirring till mixture liquidifies. Blend flour and butter with wire pastry blender. Mix well, mix in eggs, salt and yeast. Mix until dough is smooth and leaves side of bowl clean. DO NOT LET RISE. Divide into four portions and roll each out in a rectangular shape spread

with filling and roll up like Jelly Roll. Place in greased baking pans. BAKE AT ONCE in 350 oven about 30 to 45 min. or until brown.
Note: Before baking roll, prick roll top and sides with toothpick to prevent splitting.

Poppyseed Filling

- 1 pound of freshly ground poppy seeds (finely)
- 2 cups of sugar
- 1 cup BOILED milk
- 1/4 cup melted butter
- 2 teaspoons of grated lemon zest

Mix filling in bowl using only 3/4 cup of boiled milk. It should be thick. If not spreadable use the rest of milk. divide into 4 portions, one for each dough rollup.

Makes 4 Strudels.

Authentic Hungarian Quick Filled Coffee Cake from Tante Betty

Tante Betty lived with her aunt, Tante Miller who was my great aunt. They always made fresh egg coffee for company and they had company every day. There was never a time when Tante Betty's Filled Coffee Cake was not available. She could make this cake in a very short amount of time since the dough was not a yeast dough. If she did not have homemade Prune or Apricot Lekvar on hand she would always have cans of prepared pie filling ready to fill a quick coffee cake. This cake has a rich butter flavored crust that is more like a tart than a cake.

- 1 cup of butter
- 1 cup of sugar
- 2 eggs
- 2 cups flour
- 1 tsp. baking soda
- 1 tsp. baking powder

Cream butter, sugar, add eggs and beat well. Add flour and baking powder and baking soda. Spread one half of the dough into two greased 9 inch pan by buttering your hands and dipping your fingers in flour. Push the dough up around the edges to form a crust. The flour will keep the dough from sticking to your fingers. Add Lekvar filling thinned out with a little water to cover layer of dough. Or use one can of canned cherry, blueberry or apple pie filling over the dough. Watch so it does not burn. Makes two.

Streusel Mix

- 2 tsp. butter
- 1/4 cup sugar
- 1/4 cup flour

Sprinkle 1/2 of the Struesel mix on top of each cake and bake in a 350 degree oven for about 35 minutes.

Authentic Hungarian Raisin Rolled Strudel

Hungarians make many kinds of strudels. Apple Strudel made with Filo or Phylo dough is the most well know by non Hungarians. But there are other strudels made with yeast doughs that are rolled into a roll and when cut the slice shows a thick spiral of filling. That filling might be ground Poppy Seed, ground Walnut or Raisin Cinnamon. These three rolled strudels were made by my family every year at Christmas time.

A lot of visiting goes on during the Holidays. Every one visits one another to see the decorated Christmas Trees. It was a ritual to visit each other on New Year Day. All the children would receive a small coin from the uncles and grandfathers for reciting a simple poem that starts..."I wish I wish for what I do not know, but put your hand in your sack and give me something!" (this was said in German). The predecessor or "trick or treat".

A supply of strudel is baked weeks before and the cakes are wrapped and kept cold until needed. I have had some forgotten strudel turn up in the refrigerator in March, and it was as good as the day it was made. The rolled strudels start out with the same basic yeast dough, But with a difference. The yeast dough is not allowed to rise. It is mixed, made and baked in one session.

- 4 cups flour
- 4 Tbs. sugar
- 1 cup lukewarm water
- 2 eggs slightly beaten
- 2 cakes yeast regular or dry
- 1/2 cup soft butter
- 1 tsp. salt

Crumble yeast in bowl, add water and sugar stirring till mixture liquifys. Blend flour and butter with wire

pastry blender. Mix well, mix in eggs, salt and yeast. Mix until dough is smooth and leaves side of bowl clean. DO NOT LET RISE. Divide into four portions and roll each out in a rectangular shape sprinkled with raisin filling, dribble 1/4 cup of melted butter over all and roll up like Jelly Roll. Prick roll with toothpick on top and sides to keep roll from splitting while baking. Place in greased baking pans.
BAKE AT ONCE in 325 oven about 30 to 45 min. or until brown.

Raisin Filling

- 1 lb. of raisins
- 1 1/4 cups of sugar
- 1 Tbs. of cinnamon
- 1 cup melted butter

Soak raisins in hot water 5 minutes to soften raisins, drain and pat dry. Divide raisins into 4 bowls. One for each rolled strudel. To each bowl add a heaping 1/4 cup of sugar, and 1/2 tsp. of cinnamon. Toss. These cakes can be wrapped in foil and stored in the freezer after they are baked. Hope you enjoy this strudel.

Makes 4 small rolled strudels.

Authentic Hungarian Struesel Coffee Cake (Struesel Kuchen)

When ever we made Plum cake or apple cake, it was just natural to make some Streusel Coffee Cake too. The dough is the same except it has some lemon zest added. Always good to eat with coffee for breakfast. It was also the mainstay of Coffee Klatches. No household would ever be without at least Streusel Kuchen. This Streusel Coffee Cake is buttery and full of cinnamon flavor.

- 3 cups flour
- 1/4 cup of warm water
- 1 pkg. of yeast or 2 1/2 tsp. granulated yeast
- 1/2 stick of butter
- 3/4 cup scalded milk
- 3 Tbl. sugar
- 1 lemon's zest, grated
- 1/4 tsp salt
- 4 egg yolks

Heat milk to scalding, then add butter and 1 1/2 Tbs. of sugar, stir well until butter and sugar are dissolved. In small bowl, add yeast to water, with the other 1 1/2 Tbl. of sugar. Put 2 cups of flour in large bowl and add cooled milk, yeast mixture, lemon zest, eggs and salt. Beat well. Add the additional flour and work until dough comes away from sides of the bowl. Dough should be very soft and sticky. (If too thick, add a few teaspoons of warm water). Cover and let rise till double in bulk. This recipe will make 3 nine inch cake pans of Kuchen. When dough is ready, grease pan generously with butter, do not flour. Put a third of the dough in each pan, butter your hands, (otherwise the dough will stick to your hands). Using your fingers push dough to outer edges of pan, the dough will not want to stay there, but as you push into the dough, it will remain in place. Cover the dough of each cake with 1/3 of the Topping. Let rise for another 1/2 hour. Bake at 350 degrees for 30 to 35 minute or until sides and bottom are golden brown.

Topping

- 2/3 cup sugar
- 1 1/3 cups flour
- 1 1/2 Tbl cinnamon
- 1/2 lb. of butter or 2 sticks at room temperature

Cut the butter into the flour and sugar, cinnamon mix by using a wire pastry blender, as though you were making pie dough. Will be crumbly. We often double this recipe and make 6 or more. They freeze well and are nice to share.

Makes 3 cakes.

Authentic Hungarian Walnut Graham Cracker Torta (Diostorta)

Little did I know when I was 9 or 10 years old that I would develop a life long love affair with Hungarian pastry. I was old enough to be taken to Bridal Showers, Weddings, Anniversary Celebrations and Baby showers, where among our large circle of family friends it was a certainty that there would be Hungarian cookies, strudels, kipfels and tortes.

I quickly became adept at recognizing and naming the various tortes. Cherry, Dobas, Dios, Homok, Linzer, Mokka, Makos, Sacher, all beautifully baked and frosted not by caterers or bakeries but by loving mothers, grandmothers, great aunts and aunts. Guests with out a Hungarian background would marvel at these glorious creations, barely believing that they could be home made.

No bakery creation today can compare with the wonderful taste and flavor of those homemade marvels. One of my favorites was a Walnut Torte made with Graham Cracker crumbs, with a Caramel maple frosting.

- 6 egg yolks
- 2 cups sugar
- 2 Tbs. melted butter
- 2 cups milk
- 1 tsp. vanilla
- 10 oz. ground or milled walnuts
- 1 lb. of crushed graham crackers
- 2 tsp. baking powder
- 6 egg whites

Beat the yolks with sugar till thick. Add butter and vanilla, beat again. Mix crackers, nuts, baking powder

and add alternately with the milk. Fold in stiffly beaten egg whites.
Put in greased and lined two 9 x1 1/2 inch cake pans. Bake: 350 degrees. for 50 to 60 minutes.
Do not let burn.
Cool 10 minutes, remove wax paper, continue cooling.
Frost cake.

Frosting:

- 1/2 cup brown sugar
- 1/4 cup milk
- 3 Tbs. flour
- 1 tsp. vanilla
- 1/2 tsp. maple flavor
- 1/2 lb. soft butter
- 2 cups powdered sugar

Mix sugar, milk, flour and enough water to make a paste. Add vanilla and maple flavor. Cook until thick. Cream butter well, add powder sugar, a little at a time and cream. Add the cooled custard to the Butter / sugar mixture and cream until fluffy.

Authentic Hungarian Walnut Rolled Strudel (Diosbeigli)

Every celebration throughout the year will feature traditional rolled strudels. Walnut and Poppy Seed Strudels are usually served side by side. They are easy to make, the ground walnuts cooked in milk and butter have a very different flavor from the roasted walnuts usually topping rolls and cookie. Nutty flavored, rich and buttery, this is a favorite family recipe made by many generations. Always made at Christmas time and for Weddings.

- 4 cups flour
- 4 Tbs. sugar
- 1 cup lukewarm water
- 2 eggs slightly beaten
- 2 cakes yeast regular or dry
- 1/2 cup soft butter
- 1 tsp. salt

Crumble yeast in bowl, add water and sugar stirring till mixture liquifys. Blend flour and butter with wire pastry blender. Mix well, mix in eggs, salt and yeast. Mix until dough is smooth and leaves side of bowl clean. DO NOT LET RISE. Divide into four portions and roll each out in a rectangular shape spread with filling and roll up like Jelly Roll. Prick roll with toothpick on top and sides to keep roll from splitting while baking. Place in greased baking pans. BAKE AT ONCE in 350 oven about 30 to 45 min. or until brown.

Walnut filling

- 1 pound of freshly ground walnuts (finely)
- 2 cups of sugar

- 1 cup of boiled milk
- 1/4 cup melted butter

Mix filling in bowl using only 3/4 cup of boiled milk, It should be thick. If not spreadable use the rest of milk. Divide into 4 portions, one for each dough rollup. These cakes can be wrapped in foil and stored in the freezer after they are baked. Hope you enjoy this strudel.

Makes 4 small rolled strudels.

Authentic Hungarian Angel Wings Fry Cookies (Csoroge)

Angel Wings, Listys are those wonderful crispy, light as a feather fried dough cookies always made for Weddings. They look so beautiful when piled high in a pyramid on a cut crystal platter. These pastries would also be made for a Sunday dinner and served with coffee after a meal of Beef Gulyas or Chicken Paprikas. It always left traces of powdered sugar on your upper lip, and sometimes on the tip of your nose.

- 3 egg yolks
- 1 tbs. sour cream
- 1 tbs. granulated sugar
- 1 tbs. rum or whiskey
- pinch of salt
- about 1 1/2 cups sifted all purpose flour

Place in the center of a bread board one cup of flour. Make a dent or well in the center. Add the whole yolks, sour cream, sugar, rum and salt. With a fork mix until the liquids are well combined. Gradually work into the flour. The dough should be of the consistency of a noodle dough. Knead for a few minutes to make the dough smooth. Split the dough into 2 portions. On a lightly floured board roll out each section until paper thin. If you have a pie crimping wheel, use it to cut the dough into squares of 3 1/2 inches or a rectangle of 3 1/2 by 2 1/2 inches. They will have beautiful serrated edges. With a paring knife make three or four gashes about 2 to 2 1/2 inches evenly spaced. Fry in a deep fat (Lard preferred, Crisco OK) until golden brown. Drain on paper towel. Sprinkle with sifted confectioners sugar.

Authentic Hungarian Butter Balls or Little Pillows

This Christmas cookie was only made at Christmas time or for Weddings. It is a special occasion cookie. We called them Little Pillows because they looked like dainty little white pillows. The dough is butter rich and very thin, enclosing a puff of walnut filling that is soft and melt in your mouth.

When it was time to make little pillows, the whole family helped. My mother rolled out the little circles of dough between wax paper and we helped put the merangue filling on. But it was only my mother who folded them up carefully and placed them on the cookie sheet.

- 16 egg yolks
- 4 cups flour
- 1 pound of butter

Roll of wax paper cut into squares. Mix egg yolks, flour and butter together. Use hands, pastry blender or mixer. Form little balls of dough by rolling a tablespoon full of dough in your hands. Place balls of dough on a tray, cover with plastic wrap and refrigerate overnight. The next day, roll each little ball out between two small sheets of waxed paper with a rolling pin. Roll it into a thin circle. Stack the circles on their wax papers and keep chilled until you are ready to fill with meringue mixture. The filling should be made on the day you are going to bake the Pillows.

Filling:

- 1 pound of finely ground nuts, walnuts traditional
- 2 cups of sugar or 1/2 pound of sugar
- 16 egg whites
- 10 whole graham crackers

Grind or mill nuts finely. Mix nuts with all of the ground graham crackers. Beat egg whites with the sugar 1/2 cup at a time till all the sugar is used and the mix turns to meringue. Now fold in the nuts and graham cracker mixture until all is a thick filling. Put a heaping teaspoon of the filling into the center of the circle and fold over each side and tuck the ends under so it will not open, (should look like a little pillow). If the rolled out dough circle gets too warm it may be hard to peel off the wax paper, then just refrigerate the stack of rolled circles and take out a few at a time. Bake on a greased and floured cookie sheet in a moderate oven 330 degrees, for about 5 or 10 minutes or until it is lightly tan. Watch it carefully so it does not burn. Remove from baking sheet and let cool. After cool, sift powdered sugar over all. Be gentle with these, they are delicate. Store in a covered container in a cool place.

Authentic Hungarian Cream Cheese Cookies with Lekvar Filling

This Hungarian Cookie is so easy to make. It has a delicate cheese flavor that contrasts with the tart Lekvar filling. Alway made for Christmas.

- 1 16 oz. brick of cream cheese
- 1 cup of butter, softened
- 2 cups of flour

Blend in bowl with a wire pastry blender until dough forms together. Roll out like pie crust on a lightly floured surface. Cut in 2X2 inch squares. Put a dab of Apricot or Prune Lekvar in the middle of square. Take up two of the opposite corners and bring the two corners together with a squeeze over the dab of Lekvar.

Note: If you have a pie crust trimmer with a crimped wheel, you can use this to cut all the 2X2 squares. It makes a beautiful presentation. All the pastry edges have serrated edges.

Bake on a buttered and floured cookie sheet at 350 degrees for 20 minutes. Do not let burn.
Dust with Powdered Sugar.

Authentic Hungarian Kipfels (Grandma Leptich's Kipfels)

Kipfels or Kifflies were always present at any family gathering, be it a birthday, shower, anniversary, wedding or just a get together. They are made from a rich dough. Every family had their own recipe which was handed down through the generations. You could always identify whose Kipfels you were eating, either by dough flavor, fillings which contained either poppy seed, prune, apricot, cinnamon and chopped walnuts or cream cheese, or by topping or shape.

There was always an underlying competition among the women as to who's Kipfels were best. They are not large, but big enough for three or four bites. Kipfels would be stacked into pyramids. They were served with coffee after a large meal. You always had room for two or three.

These are Eastern European in origin. They have their roots in Austria, Hungary, Serbia, Croatia, Yugoslavia, Romania and Turkey. There are hundreds of variations.

- 10 cups of flour or 2 1/2 lbs.
- 3/4 lb. of butter, room temp.
- 1/4 cup of lard, room temp.
- 1/2 tsp. salt
- 5 eggs in all - 3 whole eggs and 2 yolks.
- 1 3/4 cup of warm sour cream
- 1 1/4 cup of sugar
- 2 lemon's zest grated, and reserve juice
- 2 1/2 yeast cakes or packs dry yeast

Mixture for rolling Kipfels in

- 1/2 lb. of ground walnuts mixed with 3/4 cups of granulated sugar.

Mix yeast and warm water in a small dish and proof according to yeast directions. Mix flour and shortening together in a large bowl till like pie dough, only finer. (I use my wire pastry cutter). Add all other dough ingredients including yeast mixture and work with your hands till well mixed and dough comes away from your hands and pan. If it seems dry, add the lemon juice, 1/2 lemon at a time until soft enough to mix. Let rise in a warm place till double in bulk. (I turn on the light in my oven and keep the door closed). When dough has risen, pull off about 1/4 of a cup or a small egg sized piece of dough for each cake and flatten to the size of a baby's hand (do not roll with rolling pin) but push into shape. Squeeze out about 1 tsp. of Lekvar (see recipe index) jam, and pinch up dough to cover the Lekvar jam entirely. Roll in Ground Nut mixture. Place on a greased baking pan. Let rise again for about 3/4 of and hour. Bake at 350 or moderate oven, 25 to 30 min. or till lightly brown. Cakes should be placed close together in pan, but do not crowd too closely. My kipfels look like a lot of fat little bundled up babies!

Makes 50, more or less.

Authentic Hungarian Linzerteig Cookies

Here is the original recipe for LINZERTEIG or Linzer cookies, the recipe in our family dates back about 150 years. This is the mainstay of our Christmas cookies. It is a wonderful cookie, with a hint of lemon and butter rich beyond belief. It makes a cookie that will ship well if you make them about 1/3 of an inch thick.

- 10 cups of flour
- 2 1/4 lbs. of soft butter (not melted)
- 2 lemon rinds zest grated
- 16 egg YOLKS only
- 3 cups sugar

Recipe can be doubled for big batches

- 20 cups flour
- 4 1/2 lb. butter
- 5 lemon rinds zest grated
- 30 egg YOLKS
- 6 cups sugar

Mix all ingredients in a big bowl, I use my pastry cutter (as though I were making pie crust). If your Cuisinart can handle a large amount use it. Mix until ingredients are blended and mixture can be molded in your hand. Divide mass into 3 large thick disks of dough, wrap each in saran wrap and refrigerate for 3 hours to 2 days. When ready to bake cookies, dust counter surface with flour and place one of the dough disks on flour and roll out with floured rolling pin to 1/4 to 1/3 inch thick. Cut with cookie cutters, brush top with beaten egg white wash (Egg White Wash is the white of an egg beaten with 1/2 teaspoon of water till mixed). Use a pastry brush or an European goose brush (made for this use) and sprinkle well with ground walnuts mixed with sugar. Place on a greased cookie sheet. Cookies can also be decorated with green or red sugar, multi sprinkles, etc. Just use the egg white wash to make them stick. Do not use whole nuts, they will burn. You can also roll out dough to fit in a greased baking pan, spread thick rasberry jam or apricot Lekvar over the cookie dough, and cut thin serrated strips of more dough to make a lattice design on top of the jam. Brush with egg white to give nice gloss. When the cookie dough is baked, the sheet of latticed Linzerteig is cut into 2 inch x 2 inch squares. Bake in a moderate oven. About 325 degrees. The time depends on how thick the dough is rolled out and what kind of pan you are using. Try 10 min. Do not let them burn, light tan is okay. These cookies can be stored in a cool place or freezer.

Authentic Hungarian Nut Nugget Cookies

No Wedding celebration or Christmas would be complete without these crunchy, buttery and nutty cookies. Make two kinds, Walnut Nuggets and Pecan Nuggets. They look so pretty, and taste so good.

- 1 lb. of butter, room temperature
- 10 Tablespoons of powdered sugar
- 2 cups of medium-coarse chopped nuts (Walnut is traditional but can also use Pecans)
- 2 Teaspoons of vanilla
- 4 cups of flour

In a large bowl blend the ingredients with a wire pastry blender until the ingredients form a small nugget when squeezed together. Form into nuggets by scooping out a tablespoon of dough and forming it with hand. Place on a cookie sheet and bake at 350 degrees for about 10 minutes until they start to brown around edges. Watch them so they do not burn. Cool and roll in powdered sugar. Store in cool place until needed (They are full of butter).

Makes 2 1/2 lbs. of cookies.

Authentic Hungarian Kalachki from Theresa Jerger

The Hungarians were not adverse to borrowing a good recipe when they saw one. My sister Theresa Jerger of Kalispel, Montana. adapted this recipe from an older one. It uses vegetable shortening instead of lard, and uses baking powder to make the dough lighter. This was a pastry that was made often. It is easy to make, delicious to eat and beautiful to look at. Nice to give. Makes a lot!

- 1 dry yeast added to 1/4 cups warm water
- 3/4 cup milk, scalded, let cool
- 5 cups of flour
- 1 pound of Crisco or vegetable shortening (equal to 2 cups)
- 4 egg yolks
- 3 tsp. baking powder
- 1 tsp. salt

Take flour, Crisco and mix like a pie dough. Add eggs to cooled milk and stir, then add the rest of ingredients and mix will. Refrigerate for about 3 hours. Roll out on powdered sugar. Cut into 3 X 3 inch squares. Add a teaspoon of filling (Apricot, Prune, Rasberry, Cheese, etc.). Fold over the 4 corners to the middle and seal by pushing down in center. Place on a greased and floured cookie sheet. Bake at 375 degrees for 20 to 25 minutes until golden brown. Don't let them burn. When cool sprinkle with powdered sugar.

Authentic Hungarian Kipfels or Horseshoes from Grandma Jerger

Grandma Jerger was Grandma Leptich's daughter, and my sister's mother in law. They were from the same area of Hungary as my father. They both used a similar recipe, but used different techniques to produce a different taste and look. See Grandma Leptich's Kipfels recipe story.

- 2 whole eggs and 2 yolks
- 4 cups flour
- 1 lb. sweet butter, room temp
- 2 pkgs. yeast
- 1 cup sour cream
- 1/2 cup sugar
- 1 tsp sugar to lukewarm water to dissolve yeast
- 2 lemons zest grated
- Apricot Lekvar, Prune Lekvar for filling (See Lekvar)

Put flour in large bowl. Add butter and cut in small slices and work like pie crust. I use my wire pastry blender. Take yeast and add sour cream and 1 tsp. warm water, 1 tsp. sugar and set aside. Add yeast mixture to flour and butter, also eggs and zest of 2 lemons and mix with hands until nice and smooth. Chill for 45 minutes or overnight. Take a small amount (small egg) and roll thin with rolling pin. Put filling on and roll it up with fingers, pinch both ends and curve to shape like a crescent. Place apart from one another on a greased baking pan and bake at 350 degrees for 25 to 30 minutes or until nice golden brown. Do not let burn. These can be covered with powdered sugar before serving.

Makes a lot.

Authentic Hungarian Sonya Henne Cookies

Sonya Henne was a world famous Norwegian figure skater, very popular during the early 1930's. Who named this cookie after her I do not know. If this is a traditional cookie I can't be sure, but I do know that this cookie was baked by my family for at least 65 years. So, by nestling in close association with all the Hungarian cookies, I do proclaim the Sonya Henne Cookie an authentic Hungarian cookie!

- 2 cups butter
- 1 cup brown sugar
- 4 egg yolks
- 4 cups flour
- 1 cup of milled or finely ground hazelnuts (traditional) or walnuts
- 4 egg whites beaten with 1 tsp. water

Mix dough, form into small balls, roll in beaten egg whites and then into milled hazelnuts, or walnuts. Press down to slightly flatten ball while in milled nuts. Place on a grease cookie sheet. Bake 5 minutes at 350, then take out of oven and poke a depression in the middle of the cookie and fill with Apricot or Prune Lekvar or thick red jam. Return to oven and bake for another 5 or 6 min. Do not let burn.

Authentic Hungarian Spice Cookie (Mushkazone)

One of the Hungarian cookie molds I inherited is also the oldest. Made of copper, it is in the shape of a bundle of cut wheat. As a child I thought it was a bow, but as I got older I examined it and saw that it was a sheaf of wheat. It is at least 150 years old. The only cookie made in this mold was a very old recipe for a flourless spice cookie called "Mushkazone". The cookie dough was firmly pushed into the floured mold and then carefully knocked out on a baking sheet. The cookies were baked in a low oven until it was firm. This cookie is very flavorful. The two spices, nutmeg and clove are not overpowering. You will like this spice combination. I make it every Christmas. The cookies should be stored in a cookie tin. If you do not have a mold to make these cookies, you can press the dough into a pan that has been buttered and floured on the bottom. This cookie will keep for a year in a tight tin container. It also ships well.

- 1 lb. of walnuts, ground well
- 1 lb. or 6 cups of bread crumbs, (make from dry French or Italian bread)
- 9 egg yolks
- 1/4 lb. of butter (1 stick) melted
- 1 tsp. of ground clove
- 1 tsp. ground nutmeg
- 1 lb. of sugar (2 1/2 cups)

Into mixing bowl place: Ground walnuts, bread crumbs, ground clove, ground nutmeg and sugar. Beat egg yolks with melted butter. Mix beaten egg and butter mixture into mixing bowl ingredients with a wire pastry cutter or use Cuisinart to blend. Firmly press the cookie mix flat into a pan that has been buttered and floured on the bottom. It will seem crumbly at first. (This recipe will make four 8 inch square pans or two 9 x 12 inch pans full). Make the cookie mix about 1 inch thick. With a knife or straight edged pastry board scraper, carefully cut the dough into 1 inch by 2 inch bars. Bake in a low oven about 325 degrees until firm, about 20-25 minutes. It should darken in color a little. Watch carefully. Do Not Burn! Let bars cool in pan. After they are cooled, recut with knife and keep in cookie tin.

Makes four or five 8 inch by 8 inch square pan fulls.

This recipe can be cut in half.

Authentic Hungarian Apricot and Prune Lekvar Fillings for Kipfels and Cookies

Lekvar is a very thick puree of pure fruit used in Kipfels and cookies. It is extra thick so that it will not run out of the pastries or cookies. Do not buy the canned prune and apricot fruit fillings that you will find in the food stores and suppermarkets. They are expensive for the amount you will need, and the taste cannot compare with the filling you make your self.

APPRICOT OR PRUNE LEKVAR

- 1 lb. of dried apricots **OR** pitted dried prunes
- water to just cover
- 1 cup of sugar

It is easy to make the fruit filling for Kipfels and filled cookies. Take a pound of dried fruit, either apricots or prunes, and put them in a sauce pan to cover with water and set them on the stove to cook. Do not let all the water evaporate or the Lekvar will burn. Add a little more water to keep this from happening. Once the fruit is soft add to the fruit one cup of sugar and further cook until thick. Remove from pot and puree with a food mill or a cuisinart. The puree will should be thick, not runny. If it is runny, cook till it is thick. Ladle the puree into pint sized freezer bags. These bags can be frozen until you need them or used right away. By cutting off a small corner, the bag now becomes a pastry bag which can be used to squeeze the puree onto the kipfel before it is rolled or folded up. This saves a lot of time and mess. You will want to make both prune and apricot. You will have some filling left over that be kept frozen until you need it. Then just cut off the corner of the plastic pouch and you are ready to go. Lekvar is also used as fillings for cookies.

Authentic Hungarian Cheese Filling (Turos toltelek)

Every Hungarian villager usually owned their own cow. The cow would supply the important milk, butter, cream, sour cream and cheese for the family's daily living. In the village, a young person would collect all the cows in the morning from each household, take them to the village pasture, and then return them home again for milking. Nothing was ever wasted. If you had farmers cheese you made cheese strudel or kipfels with cheese. Raisins add an extra touch.This cheese filling is for cookies and strudels to be baked. Do not use on prebaked cookies.

For Strudels

Into a large bowl blend well:

- 2 egg yolks
- 1/4 cup sugar
- 1/4 tsp. salt
- Gradually add 1 lb. (2 cups) dry cottage cheese

Mix into cheese mix:

- 1/4 cup of raisins or more if desired
- 1 tsp. lemon juice
- 1/2 tsp. fresh grated lemon zest

Spread over butter dribbled dough before rolling up strudels. For Cookies, Kipfels, Palacinta, cut recipe in half. Spoon a teaspoon full on dough before baking cookie or rolling kipfels.

Authentic Hungarian Walnut Filling for Cookies

Walnuts grow in abundance in Hungary. Walnuts are used in most nut studel recipes, kipfels, and nut cookies. The baked in a recipe walnut flavor is very different from the toasted walnut flavor. It is a more delicate and buttery flavor that lends itself to Hungarian pastries. You can never have enough walnuts on hand. Be sure you buy fresh walnuts, they can go rancid if old. Store them in the freezer or refrigerator. Always taste your walnut before using them in a recipe. You can avoid a disaster if they are rancid. This is the same filling for Walnut Strudel but halved.

- 1/2 pound of freshly ground walnuts (finely)
- 1 cup of sugar
- 1/2 cup of boiled milk
- 1/8 cup melted butter

Mix filling in bowl using only 1/4 cup of boiled milk, It should be thick. If not spreadable use the rest of milk. Use for filling Kipfils, Kalachki, or Cream cheese cookies. Can be stored in freezer. Keeps well.

Authentic Hungarian Egg Coffee

Coffee was first introduced by the Turks in the early 1500's. Hungarians have been enjoying it ever since. Where ever Hungarians mingle you will find coffee and Kipfels. Coffee for a large crowd was made in a large pot of boiling water over a hot fire. The coffee would be freshly roasted and then ground, mixed with raw eggs including the shells and salt and then dumped into the hot boiling water. It would be quickly stirred around and then the coffee would foam up. An amount of cold water would be thrown into the pot to sooth the foam and let the coffee settle down. All the egg particles and egg shells will collect with the grounds at the bottom of the pot and the coffee then is poured off into smaller coffee pots to serve. Such wonderful tasting and clear coffee you can only imagine. The aroma is mouth watering.

You can make Hungarian Coffee if you do not use a modern automatic coffee maker. The coffee makers water is just not hot enough to make the egg coagulate with the grounds. But if you use a perculator method, where the water is brought to a rapid boil, or if you use a Chemix hourglass pot where you boil the water, or if you use a plain old coffee pot where you set the pot on the fire to boil and then throw in the grounds, you too can make Hungarian Coffee.

- 1 lb. of medium ground coffee
- 1 raw egg washed
- 1/8 tsp. salt
- 1/2 cup cold water
- fresh whipped cream (optional)

Mix into one pound of coffee, the egg yolk, white and crushed egg shell. Add the salt and 1/2 cup of cold water, and mix everything together well.

Store in a covered container in the refrigerator. Use coffee mixture as you need it. Do not keep coffee mix longer than a week in refrigerator. Bring the required amount of water to a rolling boil, and spoon in your usual amount of coffee grinds (with the egg mix). Stir rapidly to distribute the grounds in the boiling water. Let it come to a boil, and have a cup of cold water handy to throw into the pot to keep it from boiling over. Turn off heat and let coffee settle to bottom of pot. Keep hot, but do not re boil.

Serve "mit Schlag" (with whip cream).

Authentic Hungarian Liptauer Cheese Spread

Unless you were rich or were an aristocratic family you did not serve appetizers. Most families ate a Hungarian cheese called Lipto. It was made of sheep milk. This cheese spread made with sheep's milk was often served in the gambling casinos in Hungary.

My Father often served this cheese spread along with a whole smoked Salami. He hung the Salami by a nail on a tree under which he and his friends would play Pinochle. The knife for cutting the Salami was stuck into the tree. The Liptauer Cheese made everyone thirsty. There would be a little wooden barrel of cold beer sitting in the shade. They played for pennies. But there would always be a lot of slapping down of cards and shouting. My Mother insisted they play outside because she didn't want all that cigar smoke and the incessant spitting that cigar smokers do.

Cream together in a bowl until well blended.

- 1/2 lb. of Lipto cheese, **OR** 1 /2 lb. Pkg. cream cheese **OR** 1/2 lb. of Feta cheese.
- 1/2 cup soft butter
- 3 Tbs. thick sour cream
- 2 anchovy fillets, mashed
- 1 tsp. capers and add to bowl with cheese mixture (Optional)

Add to cheese mixture and blend ingredients thoroughly.

- 1 Tbs. finely chopped onion
- 1 Tbs. prepared mustard
- 1 1/2 teas. paprika
- 1/2 tsp. caraway seeds smashed or bruised to release flavor
- 1/2 tsp. salt

Shape into a smooth mound and make slight indentations in mound with tines of a fork. Sprinkle with Paprika. Garnish with chopped parsley on plate.

Let flavors mingle in the refrigerator for at least 2 hours before serving.
Goes well with beer. Serve with Pumpernickle or Rye bread.

Makes1 3/4 cups of spread.

Authentic Hungarian Translyvania Krumbumballe
an old Cold Cure with Lemon and Whiskey

In my old neighborhood in "Old Town" I remember being taken to the corner Drug Store where the Pharmacist would mix up a cold remedy for us children. It was the time before all the "over the counter" drugs were available. I loved the cough syrup he made, it was called "Honey Tar". I would lick the spoon. I think the "Tar" was molasses. None of this "Honey Tar" for my father. He made this drink called Krumbumballe (if this was really its name or made up I never knew). But It was taken seriously if you had a cold and cough.

- 1 lemon sliced up thinly
- 1 cup of water
- 2 teaspoons of sugar
- 1 shot glass of whiskey

Put lemon slices, water and sugar into a small sauce pan. Cook this until the lemon is soft, do not let burn. Pour into pot, 1 shot glass of whiskey. Mix well. Ignite the whiskey and burn off the alcohol, it will burn blue, and extinguish itself. Drink the liquid down and chew the cooked lemon peel. Pile up the heaviest blankets you own on your bed, and crawl in under them and go to sleep. The idea is to sweat the cold out of your system. My Father said it always worked. As an adult, I have tried this. I must say it tastes pretty good. I can't say it did my cold any harm.

Danube Swabian History

The History of German Settlements in Southern Hungary & Danube Swabians in the Twentieth Century

by Sue Clarkson

The Danube Swabian Coat of Arms

By Hans Diplich

The History of German Settlements in Southern Hungary

by Susan Clarkson

Introduction

(All footnotes are at the end of this chapter starting on page 181)

As a child, I had often heard my grandparents talk about their home village, a German village in Austria-Hungary, but it wasn't until much later in life that I became interested in family history and began to wonder just where that village was. My grandparents had long since died and there was no one in the family to ask about it. At family gatherings, we had the same conversation over and over the village was Johannisfeld, in Austria-Hungary, but after World War I there were border changes and we didn't know what country the village belonged to. We were always confused by knowing that our grandparents spoke German, but were from Hungary and didn't understand if we were German, or Hungarian, or something else. When my uncle died in 1986, we found my grandparents' baptismal certificates among his papers, with Romanian certifying stamps in the left corner. In the local library, I was able to find Johannisfeld on an atlas-map of Romania. I was also able to find several books about the history of Romania, many of which had a chapter on "the minorities" where I found brief reference to the German settlements located in a region called the Banat.

Until that time, I had never heard of the ethnic group called Danube Swabians.[2] I had often discussed my interest with several family members. The discovery of the Danube Swabians came when my aunt, gave me a copy of the Donauschwaben[3] Kalender, printed in West Germany, which she had obtained from a friend born in Romania. Although I could not read German, I found the address of the Danube Swabian Society of the USA in the back of the book and wrote to the President. The group's bibliographer, Eve Eckert Koehler, introduced me to the English-language literature on the subject, and to sources of genealogical information, which enabled me to research my family history and to learn about the fascinating history of the Germans of the Banat region.

After my initial exploration, I traveled to Romania three times to do family history research and to learn more about the culture of the Swabians of the Banat. The following history is the story of German-speaking people who journeyed to the Banat province of Hungary during the eighteenth century, and how they came to be known as Swabians. In Romania, I learned how important it is to record the history of my Danube Swabian ancestors, because the culture is now in descendance. Due to the many waves of migration in the twentieth century, the German influence in the Banat is vanishing. In 1988, the priest at the Catholic church in Johannisfeld had been there for thirty-three years. He told me that when he first arrived there were over

2,000 Germans in the parish; in 1988 only 140 remained. Those who stayed behind are generally the older generations, the young people having left to seek a better life elsewhere, primarily in West Germany. By 1991, after the revolution which began in Timisoara and fall of Ceaucescu, only 34 Germans were left in Johannisfeld. Today, none remain, and the village is now occupied by Moldavians and Gypsies, who have moved into the houses of the former German residents.

History of German Settlements

At the end of the nineteenth century, there were more than two million Germans living in Hungary.[4] During the eighteenth century, the Habsburg monarchy of Austria,[5] which ruled Hungary at that time, had enticed Germans to emigrate to the unsettled lands of Southern Hungary, which had been devastated by over 150 years of Turkish occupation. From 1711 to *1750,* approximately 800 villages were founded in Hungary by German settlers.[6] The Banat Province[7] was one of the primary areas of settlement.

The Habsburgs had become the ruling monarchy in Hungary in 1527, following the death of King Louis II of Hungary. King Louis was killed defending Hungarian territory against the Turks (Ottoman Empire) at the Battle of Mohacs in 1526.[8] After Mohacs, the Turks dominated two-thirds of Hungary, including the Banat. The remaining portion was ruled by the Habsburgs. War with the Turks continued throughout the sixteenth and seventeenth centuries.

The Austrian Imperial Army commanded by Prince Eugene of Savoy[9] was finally successful in driving them out. A peace settlement at Karlowitz in 1699 brought Hungary, except for the Banat, under control of the Habsburg Emperor Leopold I. Later, Price Eugene captured the Banat, and the province was ceded to the Habsburg Emperor Charles VI after the Treaty of Passarovitz.[10] The Banat was considered a crown territory of the Holy Roman Empire from 1718 to 1778 and was administered from Vienna during that period.[11]

Although there had been German emigration to Hungary prior to this time,[12] the expulsion of the Turks resulted in an organized settlement program sponsored by the Habsburgs. The Habsburgs had three aims: to fortify the land against invasion, to develop farm land, and to further the Roman Catholic religion in Eastern Europe. Thus they offered Catholics of the southwest German states inducements such as free agricultural land, homesites, construction materials, livestock and exemption from taxes for several years.[13]

The colonization of the Banat was entrusted to Claudius Florimund, Count of Mercy,[14] general under Prince Eugene of Savoy.

Mercy sent agents to the Habsburg territories in the region which is now western Germany.[15] Settlers came from the regions known as Baden, Wuerttemberg, Alsace, Lorraine, the Rhineland, Westphalia, Bavaria and Swabia as well as from other areas. Although they came from various regions and spoke various dialects, the Hungarians called them Swabians, and the name came to be used in reference to all of the Germans who settled in the Danube valley. Most were poor peasants who had farmed the land of feudal lords, and who had been subjected to heavy taxation and military conscription.

The city of Ulm, in the Swabian region of the German states, was a common point of departure. From Ulm, settlers boarded boats called "Ulmer Schachtel" and sailed the Danube to Vienna, where they registered for their land. Covered wagons, which also followed the Danube, were also used for transportation. The route of the Danube took them through Budapest and into the Banat.[16]

The colonization came to be known as "der Grosse Schwabenzuge" or the "Great Swabian Trek." The majority of the migration took place in three phases which were named after their Habsburg sponsors:
1. The "Karolinische Ansiedlung," or Caroline colonization, which occurred from 1718 to 1737;[17]
2. The "Maria Theresianische Ansiedlung," or Maria Theresian colonization, which occurred from 1744-1772;[18] and
3. The "Josephinische Ansiedlung," or Josephine colonization, which took place under Joseph II from 1782 to 1787.[19]

After 1789, the government-sponsored colonization was discontinued, but some settlers continued to arrive in Hungary until 1829, after which only those with 500 Guilders cash were allowed to migrate. [20] During the colonization period, people of other nationalities also settled in the plains of the Banat. Among them were Serbs, Croatians, Bulgarians and Romanians, and to a lesser extent, Slovaks, Ruthenians, Czechs and a few French and Italians.[21]

Many of approximately 15,000 German settlers from the first colonization were killed in Turkish raids, or died from bubonic plague. Thus, the second wave of approximately 75,000 German colonists had to rebuild many of the settlements. They were successful in re-establishing the towns, but their life was filled with hard work. The third wave consisted of approximately 60,000 new German settlers who were able to increase the economic prosperity of the Hungarian farm land. The Banat region later came to be known as the "breadbasket of Europe." The hardships endured by the three groups of colonists is summarized in this verse: Die Erste hat den Tod, Der Zweite hat die Not, Der Dritte erst hat Brot, which is translated as, "The first encounters death, the second need, only the third has bread.[22] Despite the hardships, more than 1,000 German villages were established in Southern Hungary. Plans for the villages were laid out in Vienna. The towns were generally built in a square checkerboard pattern, with the Catholic church and its surrounding square in the center of the town. The style of the buildings was a modified Baroque, and came to be called "settler's Baroque." Each village, however, had slightly different designs for the decorative finishes on the buildings, and the differences are still visible today.[23]

The houses were built perpendicularly to the street, and consisted of a series of adjoining rooms, with the parlor on the end which faced the street, and sheds for domestic animals on the opposite end. Long covered porch ways extended the full length of the house. The Swabians were known for keeping their houses and gardens clean and carefully maintained. Each houseplot was surrounded by a fence, and the courtyard within the fence contained grape vines, fruit trees and the household garden.[24]

The streets in the villages were wide, and were used as pathways for community activities, such as baptism, wedding and funeral processions. Cattle were also led down the street to the common pasture in the surrounding area of the village. The streets, too, were always kept clean.[25]

Crops were grown in the fields surrounding the village. The specialty crops grown in this area were sugar beets and hemp. Other crops were wheat, corn and alfalfa. The farmers also kept horses, cattle, pigs, chickens and geese. The home gardens included grapes for eating and for wine production, vegetables, and fruits such as peaches, apricots, melons and tomatoes.[26]

In the villages, schools were built in close proximity to the church. As the settlers were allowed to bring clergy and teachers, the first school master usually came with the settlers. Teaching was done in German. Whether or not the people were pious, the social customs of the village centered around church activities. Sunday dress for the women consisted of the "tracht", or village costume, which included a distinctive dress plus decorative shawls, scarves and aprons. Each village had its own type of dress and hair style. Baptisms and weddings were festive events for family and neighbors, and included a street procession and special dinner. The major feast of the year was called "Kirchweih," the church consecration days, and was held on a Sunday in Autumn. The young men wore special hats which had been created by the young women of the village, and all took part in a procession led by a selected young couple. The day included a special mass, a festival dinner, and dancing in the street. Christmas, New Year's Day, and Easter were also special days in the villages.[27]

In the larger cities, where people were craftsmen and shopkeepers, a German middle-class and cultural life developed. Here, schools in German areas of the cities also had instruction in German. There were also German-language newspapers and magazines. Concerts, plays and balls were held, and Temeschburg was khown for its fine German theater events and other cultural activities.[28]

The Habsburg rule in Hungary, which began in *1527,* lasted for nearly four hundred years, until the dissolution of the Habsburg Monarchy in 1918. The German itninigrants, invited by Habsburg agents at the request of the Hungarian Parliament, often lived peacefully side-by-side in the cities and villages with other ethnic groups. There were many Hungarian authorities of Magyar descent, however, who resented having to accept non-Magyar rule, and the "Germanization" effect of the Habsburgs. The loyalty of the Swabians went to the Habsburgs, who were primarily responsible for freeing the land from the Ottoman Empire, and for organizing the resettlement program. [29]

Under the Habsburgs, German replaced Latin as the official language of Hungary, and German influence became very strong in the cities. In 1740, even Budapest was a predominantly German city. In the country, German peasants were the better farmers; and in the cities, many of the master craftsmen among millers, tailors, shoemakers, masons and other artisans were German. Throughout Hungary, Swabians held many positions in government offices.[30]

The Hungarian nobility wished to counteract the Swabian influence by making Magyar (Hungarian) the official language of the country, and supported scholars in the development of Magyar literature. Religion, too, was a source of conflict, since the Habsburgs wanted to advance the Roman Catholic religion in a country which had been predominantly Protestant (Lutheran, Calvinist and Unitarian.)[31]

The Habsburg Emperor Joseph II, who also ruled as King of Hungary from 1780 to 1790, attempted to reduce friction between Catholics and Protestants by passing the "Patent of Toleration" in 1781. He also introduced other reforms with the intent of improving life for the peasantry by removing them from the jurisdiction of feudal nobility, and by taxing the nobles to increase Hungary's share in supporting the cost of government. After Joseph's death, many of his reforms were reversed and Magyars began to assert greater authority. In 1844, Hungary passed the Language Act, which made Magyar the official language for government, education and religion. This was the beginning of the "Magyarization program," which was directed primarily against the German-speaking people of Hungary.[32] The Magyars wanted greater independence from Austrian rule.

In 1867, a compromise was reached with the Emperor Franz Joseph[33] which resulted in the formation of the Dual Monarchy of Austria-Hungary. In 1868, the Nationality Bill assured that all citizens of Hungary enjoyed equal rights, but also affirmed Magyar as the official language. The Educational Act of 1879 made Magyar the compulsory language of instruction, which furthered the assimilation of ethnic minorities. The Swabians were the largest minority group in Hungary, and some, particularly in the cities, became assimilated to the point of changing their family names to Magyarized versions.

Access to education beyond the village schools and to the privileges of higher social status required such assimilation, and those minorities who accepted the Magyar way of life were not subjected to discrimination. The rural Swabian villages were less affected by the Magyarization program due to their isolation, and the agrarian lifestyle there remained relatively stable for two hundred years after the settlements were established.[34]

Danube Swabians in the Twentieth Century

At the turn of the century, Hungary was a large, ethnically-diverse nation occupying over 109,000 square miles in Central and Eastern Europe. The population of more than eighteen million was 49% Hungarian (Magyar), 17% Romanian, 13% German, 13% Slovak, 4% Serbo-Croatian and 4% from other ethnic groups.[35] Since the formation of the Dual Monarchy of Austria-Hungary in 1867 under the Habsburg ruler, Franz Joseph, the Swabian peasants of the Banat had enjoyed a period of economic prosperity due to the thriving agricultural economy of the region. At this time, most Swabians were not politically aware or nationality-conscious, and they were proud of their children who had moved to urban areas and found success via Magyarization.[36]

Land ownership was necessary for making a good living in agriculture, and the Swabian Germans practiced the inheritance custom known as "Anerberecht," in which land holdings were inherited by the first-born son, keeping farm sizes large and intact. Other sons were forced to earn a livelihood as landless farm workers, or in other professions. This custom differed from the Magyar practice of dividing farm lands among their sons, which resulted in increasingly small parcels with each subsequent generation. Large tracts of land in Hungary were still held in possession by the upper class and the Roman Catholic Church, leaving very little farm land for sale, and at very high prices. As the population continued to grow, lack of available land eventually led to wide-scale emigration, primarily to the United States and Canada, but also to other countries. Between 1899 and 1911, over 197,000 Germans left Hungary. For many, the goal was to earn enough money to return to Hungary and buy land, and some did return, but most stayed in their new countries.[37]

Other factors contributed to emigration from Hungary. In America, industry was expanding rapidly, and steamship lines and manufacturers sent agents to the villages to recruit factory workers.[38] Compulsory military service caused some young men to leave. Under Parliamentary law, military service began when a man reached the age of 21. After three years of active service, men were transferred to the "Reserve," where they could be recalled until reaching 43 years of age.[39] Others were tired of the heavy taxation which resulted in poverty and inequality for the peasant class. Emigration continued in the years immediately following World War I.

World War I was a turning point for Austria-Hungary and its ethnic groups. Even before the war was over, nationalities within Austria-Hungary were eager for independence. In October 1918, the Czechoslovak Republic was declared and the Yugoslav National Council proclaimed independence from the Dual Monarchy. The Hungarian Republic was formed in November and in December, the Romanian National Assembly declared unity with the geographical regions known as the Banat and Transylvania. When the war ended, the Habsburgs were no longer in power, and Austria-Hungary had been dissolved. Revised final boundaries for Hungary were formed at the Treaty of Trianon in June, 1920, and this resulted in the loss of two-thirds of her former territory. Land in Transylvania and most of the Banat was awarded to Romania. Yugoslavia gained land in Southern Hungary, including a strip of the western Banat. Czechoslovakia became a new country fashioned out of former Hungarian territory.[40] The Swabian villagers whose families had lived in Hungary for almost 200 years now found themselves in three different countries.

In post-Trianon Hungary, the Germans, by default, became the largest minority group, because the people from the other minority groups were now citizens of other countries. Although the post-war treaties contained clauses which protected the rights of ethnic minorities, Magyarization continued to put pressure on Germans. In part as a counter-reaction, and also stemming from contact with Germany as a result of the war, cultural awareness began to develop among young, educated Swabians in urban areas.

German cultural societies such as the "Ungarischer Deutscher Volksbildungsverein" (UDV, Educational Association of the German Peoples in Hungary) were founded. A later group, the "Volksbund der Deutschen in Ungarn", (VDU, Union of Germans in Hungary), which was more political than cultural, became subsidized by the German National Socialist party (Nazis), who were eager to promote their concept of "Herrenvolk", or "Great German Folk". The VDU was favorably received by the majority of youth under 35, but was rejected by most of the elder "Swabians".[41]

Romania inherited large numbers of ethnic German citizens as a result of World War I. Here, freedom was granted to the Germans to conduct school lessons and church services in their own language. A cultural association called the "Verband der Deutschen in Rumaenien" (Union of Germans in Romania) was founded in 1921. In Yugoslavia, Germans set up schools where teaching was done in the German language, and formed the "Schwaebisch-Deutschen Kulturbund" (Swabian-German Cultural Union). The National Socialist party was also able to gain influence in these countries, as they had done in Hungary.[42]

In the period between the wars, the lifestyle of Germans in rural villages in all three of the countries remained much the same, and the isolated villagers were much less affected by the political concerns which arose in the cities. However, the rise of Hitler in Germany and the outbreak of World War II forced even rural Swabians to become conscious of their status as ethnic Germans. Hungary and Romania were initially aligned with Germany, although they both changed alignment later, while Yugoslavia sided with the Allies.

In Hungary, with the full sanction of the Hungarian government, Swabians could enlist either in the Hungarian army or the German army. The National Socialistss recruited Hungarian Germans by bringing them into Germary for youth camps, summer schools and sports programs, where they were indoctrinated with propaganda. Many youths volunteered freely for the German army to avoid the discrimination they were sure to receive in the Hungarian army. The German army encouraged those who had Magyarized their names to change them back. Many were recruited to the Waffen Schutz Staffel (Waffen SS, the military militia). In Romania, Swabians could also enlist in the Germany army and remain Romanian citizens, and more than ten percent of the German population did so.

Yugoslavian Germans also enlisted in the Waffen SS, many of them into the all- Swabian Prince Eugene Division, named after the Austrian military hero who had freed Hungary from the Turks. After Germany overran Yugoslavia and occupied the country in 1941, Yugoslavians of German descent were forced into the German army. Feelings among Swabians, however, were not unanimously in favor of the National Socialist party, and there were as many who resisted the movement as there were who supported it.[43]

As German defeat became imminent, German military leaders initiated plans to evacuate ethnic Germans from the many Eastern European countries in which they lived. In Hungary, many refused to leave the only homeland they had ever known, but some 50,000, primarily those most closely associated with Nazi Germany, did leave in convoys of horse-drawn peasant wagons. The Soviet communists took control of the country, and in some Swabian villages, most of the adult German men and women who remained were deported to forced labor camps in the Soviet Union. Those who did not die in the harsh conditions in the camps were returned to Hungary in 1946, but found that they were no longer welcome. In 1945, German-owned land had been seized by the government without compensation, and non-Magyarized Germans had been expelled as traitors. Germans were considered non-Magyarized if they had listed German as their nationality or as their mother tongue on the latest census, if they had changed Magyarized names back to German, or if they were members of a cultural association of the Waffen SS. The expulsions took place in 1946, and resulted in 170,000 Germans being transported to the American Zone of West Germany, and 50,000 to the Soviet Zone in East Germany.[44]

The Russians liberated Romania from the Germans in 1945. About 100,000 Swabians had left Romania when the Soviet troops began to arrive. There were no reprisals or expulsions in Romania, but property of German-speaking citizens was confiscated without compensation. Under Soviet authority, 75,000 adult German men and women were deported to labor camps in the Russian Ukraine. The 85% who survived the difficult conditions in the camps were released from 1945-1951. About half of those released did not return to Romania, but went instead to West Germany, East Germany or Austria.[45]

In Yugoslavia, 60% of the Swabians left the country in horse-drawn carts with the retreating German army as Soviet troops invaded. Those who remained were declared traitors, and were subjected to cruel and harsh treatment due to their association with the German soldiers who had occupied their country during the war. Since 1941, the German occupation had created high levels of resentment among the predominantly Serbo-Croatian population. The German Army had executed thousands of Yugoslavian hostages in retribution for the killing and wounding of German soldiers during the occupation. The result was that in 1944, Germans were stripped of citizenship, and their property, was confiscated. Approximately 27,000 to 37,000 were deported to the Soviet Union, and others were placed into concentration camps which had been made from Swabian villages, resulting in 35,000 to 45,000 children being separated from their parents. Thousands died in the camps from starvation, malnutrition and disease, but other thousands escaped and went to Germany. The camps were finally closed in 1948, and from *1952* to *1955*, the survivors were resettled in Germany by the International Red Cross. Only ten per cent of the pre-war German population remained in Yugoslavia.[46]

Prior to World War II, approximately 1.5 million Danube Swabians lived in Hungary, Romania and Yugoslavia. The result of war deaths, expulsions, deaths in labor and concentration camps, and emigration was a reduction of two-thirds of that number. In 1983, only 550,000 Swabians were estimated to remain (270,000 in Hungary, 250,000 in Romania, and 30,000 in Yugoslavia). Of the approximately one million refugees who went to Germany and Austria, about 250,000 later emigrated to other countries, including the United States, Canada, Australia, France and the South American countries of Argentina, Brazil and Venezuela. Emigration still continues particularly from Romania, even though it is difficult to get permission from the government to leave.[47]

The events which forced the Swabians from their homeland triggered a heightened awareness of their unique ethnic identity. In Austria, there now exists the Danube Swabianmuseum, the Danube Swabian archives, and the "Haus der Donauschwaben" at Salzburg. In Germany, many cities have active Danube Swabian organizations, and Danube Swabian newspapers and other special publications exist. In Sindelfingen, the Haus der Donauschwaben has cultural exhibits and a research archive. There is also a genealogical association which is totally dedicated to genealogical research on Danube Swabian families.

Ethnic clubs also exist in Australia, South America, the United States and Canada. Many of the clubs sponsor special events commemorating their cultural history. In the U.S., the national Danube Swabian Association of the USA, Inc., was founded in *1956*, and has its base in Milwaukee, Wisconsin.[48]

The eventual result of the emigration of the Danube Swabians from Hungary, Romania and Yugoslavia is the disappearance of their cultural influence in the region. Those Germans who remained in Yugoslavia are already "invisible" even though the past is still evident in the architectural appearance of the villages. The remaining German populations in Hungary and Romania are too small to make a cultural impact. Since so many members of younger generations have left, the number of German children being born continues to diminish.

Although the emigrants continue to preserve memories of their cultural heritage, first-hand knowledge of the traditions will disappear. Change is inevitable in all societies, and it is fortunate that so many associations have been founded in so many countries to preserve the history of the Danube Swabians.

Footnotes

[1] The History of German Settlements in Southern Hungary by Susan Clarkson, was reproduced in this book with kind permission from the author and The Federation of East European Family History Societies (FEEFHS), who jointly hold the copyright for this text. This version also includes an introduction by the author, along with footnotes to document the information, explain the historical context and provide further detail.

The Federation of East European Family History Societies (FEEFHS) was founded in June 1992 by a small dedicated group of American and Canadian genealogists with diverse ethnic, religious and national backgrounds. FEEFHS represents over one hundred seventy organizations as members from twenty seven U.S. States, the five western Canadian provinces and fourteen countries, representing virtually every East or Central European group that has an existing genealogy society in North America, a growing number of Central and East European Societies and a growing group of world-wide organizations.

FEEFHS headquarters is in Salt Lake City, a natural place for a genealogy Federation. Access to the world's largest genealogical repository and the associated genealogy infrastructure is only part of the reason for this location. However FEEFHS is nonsectarian. It has no connection with the Family History Library nor the Church of Jesus Christ of Latter-day Saints (LDS). FEEFHS greatly appreciates the LDS contribution to family history in collecting, filming and sharing genealogy records.

If you have any questions or would like to join FEEFHS, the permanent address is:
FEEFHS, P.O. Box 510898, Salt Lake City, Utah 84151-0898.

FFEFHS Web Site address on the Internet is http:/feefhs.org FEEFHS Webmaster John Movius can be e-Mailed at: feeths@feeths.org

[2] The term "Danube Swabian" is used to describe people of German descent who emigrated to the Danube valley region of Hungary. According to Katherine Frey, in *The Danube Swabians, A People with Portable Roots,* p. 9, the term was coined by Dr. Robert Sieger in 1922 at the University of Graz in Austria. It was used to differentiate between ethnic Germans of Eastern Europe, and true Swabians who live in the Swabian area of West Germany. Another term, "Danube Germans", is also used interchangeably with Danube Swabians.

[3] "Donauschwaben" is the German word for Danube Swabians. The Danube River is "Donau", and Swabians is "Schwaben." The Donauschwaben Kalender is an almanac-book containing calendar pages with listings of Catholic and Evangelical holy days, and phases of the moon. The bulk of the book consists of articles and photographs of Danube Swabians in their old and new homelands. It is published as a means of preserving information about the culture of the Danube Swabian people who left Hungary, Romania and Yugoslavia, and now live in Germany or other countries.

[4] The population statistic quoted is from Robert William Seton-Watson, *Treaty Revision and the Hungarian Frontiers,* p. 26 It is based on the Hungarian Statistical Year Book. Seton-Watson believed that the figures under-represented the population of non-Magyar ethnic groups in order to support the Magyarization program, which will be discussed later in this manuscript.

[5] According to Geoffrey Barraclough (Ed.), *The Times Atlas of World Histoiy,* pp. 150 and 309, the Habsburgs were a major European royal dynasty from the fifteenth to the twentieth centuries. The reign of the Habsburgs began in Austria in 1278. In 1452, the Habsburg King of Germany, Frederick V, was named Holy Roman Emperor of the German Nations. In the early sixteenth century, the Empire included vast territories in what is now known as Spain, Netherlands, Germany, much of Italy, Austria, part of Hungary, and other smaller possessions. After the death of Charles V in *1558,* the house split into the Spanish line, which later died out, and the Austrian line. The Austrian line remained in power in Central Europe until the death of Franz Joseph I in 1916, and the subsequent dissolution of the monarchy in 1918 after the abdication of Charles I of Austria.

[6] This quote on the number of German villages settled in Hungary is taken from Thomas Spira, *German-Hungarian Relations and the Swabian Problem,* 1977) p. 2.

[7] According to Charles Upson Clark, *United Romania,* p. 112, the Banat Province had as its boundaries the Marosch River on

the north, the Theiss River on the West, the Danube River on the South, and the Carpathian mountains on the East. The area of the province was approximately 11,000 square miles, and is larger than Vermont, but smaller than Maryland.

[8] Mohacs is a Hungarian city on the Danube south of Budapest. The Battle of Mohacs is briefly discussed by Harold W. V. Temperley in his Introductory Essay to *Hungary in the Eighteenth Century* by Henry Marczali, p. xxxix.

[9] Prince Eugene of Savoy (1663-1736) was a Frenchman who became the commander of the Austrian Army. Savoy is a region in southeast France.

[10] Information on these treaties is included by Temperley in Marczali, *Hungary in the Eighteenth Century,* pp. x'i-lvii. Karlowitz is located on the Danube River northwest of Belgrade, Serbia. It is now named Sremski Karlovici. Passarovitz is located southeast of Belgrade near the Danube. It is now named Pozarevac.

[11] From Anton Tafferner, Josef Schmidt and Josef Volkrnar Senz,*The Danube Swabians in the Pannonian Basis, a New German Ethnic Group,* p. 13.

[12] According to Geza Paikert, *The Danube Swabians,* pp. 10-li, the first wave of German immigration to Hungary occurred in the eleventh century at the invitation of St. Stephen, the first King of Hungary, who wanted German monks, preachers, knights, traders and craftsmen. Another organized program occurred during the twelfth century under King Geza II, who invited Germans to occupy the Transylvanian region. These Germans came to be known as the 'Transylvania Saxons,' even though they emigrated from the Rhineland area of Germany, not from Saxony.

[13] Ibid, *p. 25.*

[14] Count Mercy (1666-1734) was descended from a royal family of Lorraine. For more information, see Taffemer, et at, *Danube Swabians in the Pannonian Basin,* p. 13.

[15] Only in the recent history of Europe have boundaries of countries been strictly-defined, and even after this definition took place, boundaries have fluctuated as the result of various wars and agreements. According to *Gene* Gurney, *Kingdoms of Europe: An Illustrated Encyclopedia of Ruling Monarchs from Ancient Times to the Present,* pp. 256, 262-264, the region known as Germany prior to World War II had been called Imperial Germany for the period 481 to 962. From 982 to 1806, the territory, which also included Austria at that time, was called tlie Holy Roman Empire of German Nations. The Holy Roman Empire was composed of various kingdoms, duchy, principalities and bishoprics. The Holy Roman Empire ended in 1806, and the German nations were not united until 1867, when a North German Confederation under Prussian control was declared. German states in the southern region, excluding Austria, later joined the confederation, and the Second Reich was declared in 1871 (the first Reich was the Holy Roman Empire). The Second Reich was ruled by the royal family known as the Hohenzollerns. The

Hohenzollerns abdicated in 1918, and Germany became a republic.

[16] From Kathleen Frey, *The Danube Swabians, a People with Portable Roots,* p. 16.

[17] According to Temperley, in Marczali, *Hungary in the Eighteenth* Century, p. lx-lxi, Charles VI (1685-1740) ruled from 1711 to 1740. He promulgated the Pragmatic Sanction in 1723, which guaranteed succession of the throne of Austria to a female, which enabled his daughter, Maria Theresa, to become Queen after his death.

[18] According to Barraclough, *Times Atlas,* p.314, Maria Theresa (1717-1780) reigned over the Habsburg lands from 1740-1780, and was considered to be one of the most capable of the Habsburgs. Her husband, Francis I, was elected Holy Roman Emperor in 1745 and held that title until his death in 1765.

[19] According to Barraclough, *TimesAtlas,* p.314, Joseph 11 (1741-1790) became Holy Roman Emperor in 1765 after the death of his father, Francis I. He succeeded to the Habsburg lands in 1780 after the death of his mother, Maria Theresa.

[20] From Michael Bresser, *The Danube Swabians, Biography of a People from Inception to Dispersal,* pp. 3-5

[21] From Taffemer, et al, *Danube Swabians in the Pannonian Basin,* pp. 7-8.

[22] This version of the verse is from Frey, A *People with Portable Roots,* p. 24.

[23] From Nikolaus Engelman, *The Banat Germans,* translated from German by John Michels, p. 28.

[24] Ibid., pp. 28, 41.

[25] Ibid., pp. 34-35.

[26] From Tafferner, et al, *Danube Swabians in the Pannonian Basin,* pp. 15-16.

[27] From Engelman, *The Banat Germans,* pp. 24, 49, 58, 65, 73-77.

[28] Ibid., pp. 19-20.
[29] From Paikert, *The Danube Swabians,* pp. 12, 16, 17, 27.

[30] From Marczali, *Hungary in the Eighteentlz Century,* pp. 208-209.

[31] Ibid., pp. 229, 263.

[32] From Frey, A People with Portable Roots, p. 24.

[33] According to Barraclough, *Times Atlas,* p. 307, Franz Josef (1830-1916) ruled from 1848 to 1916. His nephew and heir to the throne. Franz Ferdinand, was assassinated in Sarajevo in 1914, an incident which led to the outbreak of World War I.

[34] From Frey, *A People with Portable Roots,* pp. 25-26.

[35] The figures are from G. Freytag, *Osterreich-Ungarn 1914,* (Vienna; Freytag-Berndt & Artaria, 1975), a reproduction of a 1914 map of Austria-Hungary.

[36] From Geza C. Paikert, *The Danube Swabians.* pp. 32, 46.

[37] From Adam Wandruska. *The House of Habsburg. Six Hundred Years of a European Dynasty,* pp. 32-33, 35-36.

[38] From Michael Bresser, *The Danube Swabians, Biography of a People from Inception to Dispersal,* p. 13.

[39] From Zoltan Kramer, *From the Danube to the Hudson,* p. 89.

[40] From Robert William Seton-Watson, *Treaty Revsion and the Hungarian Frontier,* pp. 17-19.

[41]From Paikert, *The Danube Swabians,* pp. 90-91, 116-130.

[42] Ibid., pp. 248-50, 265-69.

[43]Ibid., pp. 144-46, 253-54, 276, 280. Paikert notes that the Waft'en SS, the military militia, must be differentiated from the regular SS, a political militia not part of the army.

[44] Ibid., pp. 186-7, 195-200, 205-08.

[45] Ibid., pp. 256-59.

[46] Ibid., pp. 276-76, 281-290. The largest camps were at Gakovo, Kruschevlje, Jarek and Rudolfsgrad. In Rudolfsgrad alone, which held some 33,000 Swabians,almost 10,000 died between October, 1945 and March, 1948. There were also other camps at Stefansfeld, MoIidorf, Brestowatz., Kathreinfeld, Filipovo, Sekitsch, Neusatz, Futog, Guduritz, Karlsdorf and Valpovo.

[47] From Jacob Steigerwaid, *Donauschwabische Gedankenskizzen aus USA - Reflections of Danube Swabians in America,* p. 5.

[48] From Jacob Steigerwaid, *Tracing Romania's Heterogeneous German Minority from its Origins to Diaspoara,* p. 42.

Bibliography

Barraclough, Geoffrey, ed. *The Times Atlas of World History.* Maplewood, N.J.: Hammond, Inc. 1984.

Bresser, Michael. *The Danube Swabians: Biography of a People from Inception to Dispersal.* Philadelphia: Danube Swabian Association, n.d.

Clark, Charles Upson. *United Romania.* New York: Arno Press & thc New York Times, 1971.

Engelmann, Nikolaus. *The Banat Germans* Translated by John Michels. Bismarck, ND: Univ of Mary Press, 1987.

Frey, Katherine Stenger. *The Danube Swabians: A People with Portable Roots.* Belleville, Ont., Canada: Mika Publ. Co., 1982.

Gurney, Gene. *Kingdoms of Europe: An illustrated Encyclopedia of Ruling Monarchs from Ancient Times to the Present.* New York: Crown Publishers, 1982.

Kramar, Zoltan. *From the Danube to the Hudson: US Ministerial Dispatches on Immigration From the Habsburg Monarchy:] 850-1900.* Foreward by Steven Bela Vardy. Program in the East European and Slavic Studies Publication Number 9. Atlanta: Hungarian Cultural Foundation, 1978.

Koehler, Eve Eckert. *Seven Susannahs: Daughters of the Danube.* Milwaukee: Danube Swabian Societies of the US and Canada, 1976.

Macartney, C.A. *Hungary: A Short History* Edinburgh Univ Press, 1962.

Marezali, Henry. *Hungary in the Eighteenth Centuty.* Introductory essay by Harold W. V. Temperley. Cambridge: Cambridge Univ Press, 1910; reprinted., New York: Arno Press and the New York Times, 1971.

Paikert, Geza C. *The Danube Swabians: German Populations in Hungary, Romania and Yugoslavia and Hitler's Impact on their Patterns.* The Hague: Martinus Nijhoff, 1967.

Seton-Watson, Robert William. *Treaty Revision and the Hungarian Frontiers.* London: Eyre and Spottiswood Ltd., 1934.

Spira, Thomas. *German-Hungarian Relations and the Swabian Problem,* Eastern European Quarterly. New York: Columbia Univ Press, 1977.

Steigerwald, Jacob. *Donauschwaebisches Gedankenskizzen aus USA - Reflections of Danube Swabians in America.* Winona, MN: Translation and Interpretation Service, 1983.

Steigerwald, Jacob. *Tracing Romania's Heterogeneous German Minority from its Origins to the Diaspora.* Winona, MN: Translationa and Interpretation Service, 1985.

Tafferner, Anton; Schmidt, Josef; and Senz, Josef Vokmar. *The Danube Swabians in the Pannonian Basin, a New German Ethnic Group.* Milwaukee: Danube Swabian Association, USA, Inc., 1982.

Wandruska, Adam. *The House of Habsburg: Six Hundred Years of a European Dynasty.* Translanted from German by Cathleen and Hans Epstein. New York: Doubleday & Co., Inc., 1964.

Danube Swabian Coat of Arms
By Hans Diplich

The Imperial Eagle is a symbol of the Holy Roman Empire under Germanic kings. The wavy line symbolizes the Danube River, on which or along which, the German settlers traveled to Hungary. The crescent moon is the symbol of Islam, representing the Turkish occupation of Europe during the 17th and 18th centuries. The sun is the symbol for Christ. The fortress represents the city of Temeschburg (Timisoara). It's six towers represent the six main settlement regions for the Danube Swabians: Swabian Turkey, Slavonia, Syrmia, Batschka, Banat and Sathmar.

The fortress stands on the fertile farm land made arable and productive by the Danube Swabians. The inscription reads, "The Danube Swabians - Forever Free and Undivided." (This motto probably refers to the fact that the Donauschwaben were free persons and no longer peasants bound to a lord. "Undivided" refers to their feeling of being "one people" despite being separated into different countries after WWI and after the diaspora around the world after WWII.)

The coat of arms of the Danube Swabians was originated by Hans Diplich in 1950.

Alphabetical Recipe Index

Recipe Category Index

I Hope You Enjoyed June Meyer's Authentic Hungarian Heirloom Recipes

June Meyer can be reached for comments at:
978 Maple Ct. Deerfield, IL 60015 USA

Or you can E-mail me at:
june4@interaccess.com

And please check out my Web Page at:
http://homepage.interaccess.com/~june4/

Last Revised 10/11/99

June Meyer's Authentic Hungarian Heirloom Recipes Book Order Form

To order extra copies of this book send a check or money order made payable to June Meyer (**in US funds only**) per book to:

June Meyer
978 Maple Ct. Deerfield, IL 60015
USA

Please include your name, address, state, zip, phone number and E-mail address.

If you are in the Continental U.S. the book is **$20.00** including shipping costs.
If you are in Illinois, the cost is **$21.75** which includes state tax and shipping costs.
If you are in Canada, the cost is **$25.00 (in US funds)** including shipping and handling.

All others please write or E-mail for S&H rates E-mail June Meyer at:
june4@interaccess.com